Broken Beyond Repair

by
Abi Dyer

Chapter One

Peering anxiously at my reflection in the highly
polished steel door, I scrutinised my face and body.
The outfit that I had chosen so carefully, stepped out
in so confidently only an hour before, was a mistake.
I frowned. Back home, twirling in front of my
bedroom mirror, I'd felt demure yet desirable. The
dress had skimmed seductively, neckline and hem
ending at just the right level of 'hint of flesh/not too
much.' Now? It clung maliciously, highlighting every
lump and bump of flesh that no amount of calorie
counting had ever managed to reduce. I wasn't slim
enough, young enough, or pretty enough for this
dress. What had I been thinking?! My hair had frizzed
in the drizzle, and the red lipstick was most definitely
too much. *And* had managed to stain my teeth.
Cursing, rubbing furiously at the offending splodge of
scarlet with my index finger, I made a decision. Sod
it! I was going home.

   I glanced up at the relatively tasteful fake
Victorian clock that hung weightily from the ceiling.
Its ornate hands moved relentlessly towards our
appointed hour. Ten brief minutes to go. Time enough
to make my escape. I'd go back to the car, text him an
excuse. Car trouble. Sudden illness. Family
emergency. All very plausible …he'd believe me,

right? We could do it some other time. I sighed. Cursed my cowardice. If I left now, there wouldn't be 'some other time.' This was a 'now or never' situation. Come on, woman! Get yourself together! Faint heart and all that. I took a breath and forced myself to sit down on one of the chilly steel seats. Winced. Definitely not designed with comfort in mind. What was that, mesh? Who would design a chair and go for metal mesh as the ideal material? Shifting uncomfortably, I crossed my legs and attempted an air of nonchalance. Almost as if meeting handsome strangers in railway stations was something I did every weekend.

We'd met online. I was browsing one of those dating sites that offered up potential mates: a catalogue of faces, all trying to attract *someone.* Perhaps Mr Right, Mr Right Now, Mr Once-And-Then-Never-Again. What was *I* looking for? I wasn't sure... nothing fleeting. No judgement, each to their own, but I'd been there, tried it out for size, bought the T-shirt, and found it had left me feeling empty. And a bit sad. So, I knew what I *didn't* want, but as for what I *did* want? Not so clear. I'd know when I found it. Rely on instinct. Gut feeling. Once I'd discounted the photos of men posing next to their car/yacht/solid gold toilet (too materialistic), men without shirts (too vain), and men hanging from a

2

mountain top (too outdoorsy), there had been very little left to choose from. Swipe, swipe, swipe…hang on! Now, *there* was a man who knew how to take a selfie! His photos were matinee idol perfection—deep brown eyes, neat facial hair, strong white teeth… the kind of man you hoped would be as charming as he looked. I'd made the first move—subtle with just a hint of sauce—and hoped he'd respond. Not only did he respond (score!), but he did indeed seem to be as charming as his photos (double score!). Along with the charm, there was humour, intelligence, and a hint of eccentricity. Over the next few weeks, we began with a couple of messages a day that swiftly grew into full-blown text volleys—evenings filled with joyful back-and-forth messaging, full of genuine warmth. I'd felt a connection and hoped he did too. He was a freelance writer—film and music reviews mostly—who spent his spare time volunteering for Oxfam. He lived alone with a cat he'd rescued from a grim alleyway—a single mother of six. After rehoming her brood, he took her in, and she became his best bud. His accounts of her antics were sweet, endearing; showed a gentle, nurturing side to his nature. Something that many men may have struggled to reveal. No hint of machismo. Refreshing. I'd begun to look forward to our nightly messaging sessions with excitement and was

3

pleasantly surprised when the usual sexting failed to appear. Oh, he was flirtatious, but just enough to let me know he was attracted to me. I wasn't used to that. Most men were telling you what they wanted to do to you by the second message. Sometimes sooner. He seemed different. Perfect. So, I suggested we meet. IRL, as the kids say. And so here I was.

And then, there *he* was.

I'd chosen a seat that would allow me to watch his approach before he got a good look at me. Stepping off the train, he moved with casual confidence. Taller than I expected, he was achingly cool in leather jacket and jeans, wearing a hat that I later learned had belonged to his much-loved grandfather. I tried to arrange myself attractively as he approached and attempted a relaxed smile.

His eyes swept the room, then fixed on me. Sought out my own and held contact without breaking. Wearing an eager grin that grew broader as he approached, he quickened his pace, until he there he was. Towering over me, obscuring the harsh lighting so I was sitting in comfortable shadow. Before I could trot out my well-rehearsed hellos, he reached down for my hands and pulled me upwards until we were standing toe-to-toe. Not quite face to face, more face to (pleasingly broad) chest

"Where are we going? Your choice! Of course,

4

it's your choice, your hometown, never been here before! Well, once…to the theatre, I think? There is one here, yes? A nice little Victorian one, all velvet curtains and those golden cherubs. Putti maybe? We'll have to go together sometime! Anything good on do you know?"

He was gabbling, clearly nervous, making no attempt to hide his excitement. Actually, I was relieved he was so vocal. It saved me from having to talk - and potentially say something ridiculous. I really didn't want to put a foot wrong.

We headed for one of my favourite pubs - traditional and romantic I thought: working gas lights, red leather upholstery, dark polished wood. He'd grabbed my hand before we left the station and held it firmly as we walked. His stride was much longer than mine ; I had to work hard to keep up without tripping. I'd worn heels. Not my usual choice, but you know— *making an effort*. At one point, he stopped and twirled me around twice, almost knocking me off my ill-considered footwear. Disaster averted! He caught me around the waist, and held me briefly to him, before walking on as if nothing had happened. Yes, definitely eccentric! But I liked it.

"Wow, I'm impressed!" Initially, I thought he was referring to my heel-balancing skills —no small feat negotiating a 1 in 5 whilst wearing 4 inchers— but it was the pub he was impressed by. Nestling at the bottom of the hill, an 18th-century splendour sporting leaded glass windows and highly polished heavy wooden doors. Not that I felt the weight of those doors—he darted ahead of me and held them open with an exaggerated flourish. I half expected a little bow, but was just as flattered by his quick wink. Tottering past him and making gratefully for one of the leathery horseshoe-shaped seating areas, I sank into deeply buttoned butter soft upholstery with as much grace as I could muster. A well-dressed woman sitting opposite caught my eye and gave me a wry smile, accompanied by a slight eyeroll. I wondered if she was waiting for her date to arrive. Would she be as happy with her choice as I was with mine?

He was soon by my side, fussing over coasters for drinks, splitting open a bag of crisps for us to share and settling so closely that the outsides of our thighs pressed against each other. I blushed at the contact: simultaneously shy and excited.

Heaving the door open, a man entered, bringing the total number of lunchtime drinkers to four. The three of us watched him as he peered into the dimly lit room, smiled a relieved little smile, and approached the lone woman.

"Hello! You're early!"

She raised an eyebrow.

6

"No, not really. *I* was on time." Heavy emphasis on the "*I*".

Ouch! I caught my date's eye, and we shared a secret smile: slightly smug. Lit by dancing gaslight, two couples were competing in the dating game. One couple were clear favourites to lift the trophy.

We fell into easy conversation, building on what we'd learned about each other over the last few weeks, laughing again at jokes we'd made online—private jokes that only two people who knew each other well would understand. I could feel the connection between us growing: unforced and organic.

Two hours flew by in easy conversation before we felt the need to take ourselves back into the sunlight. As we got up to leave, the man opposite leant across.

"Can I just say, I love your outfit! "he gushed. His date's expression went from chilly to glacial. Yup, definitely blown it!

We held in our giggles until we were safely outside.

"He was talking to you, right?"

"Perhaps. Although you are looking pretty sharp!"

He smiled, spinning on the spot for me with arms outstretched. Seemingly oblivious to the amused glances thrown our way.

"You think? "His voice became low,

conspiratorial. "I saved this jacket for today. Put it aside for myself as soon as it came into Oxfam. Not strictly allowed, but.... I just couldn't resist."

"You broke charity shop rules?" I clutched at my throat in mock horror.

"Hey, I paid the asking price. Every last penny!"

"Well, it was money well spent. You look hot."

Aaagh! So much for playing it cool. I blushed, embarrassed, but he smiled broadly at the compliment and took my hand, giving it a squeeze and a quick caress with his thumb. I relaxed.

There was no question of us heading back to the station yet. We walked, talked, laughed and smiled into each other's eyes, until hand-in-hand became arms around waists. Our feet found their way to The Gardens- a beautifully landscaped public park, busy with beds of nodding flowers, lovingly tended trees, couples and families all enjoying the fine weather. The agony of heels forced me to request a seat for a while, so we chose one of the 'In Memoriam' benches. This one read '*In Memory of Lilly Mackenzie (1916-1993) who liked to sit down.*' I could relate. My feet were hot with approaching blisters-not that I was going to admit it. We were not yet at the stage where I could kick off my shoes and walk barefoot in the park. I would soldier on and deal with the consequences of choosing vanity over practicality later.

Fading sunlight signalled to us that it was time to go. We walked reluctantly back to the station, his stride much slower now. There were a few precious minutes left before his train would pull in. we paused under the fake Victorian clock -Our Clock -and we kissed. Our first.

"Same time next week?"

I nodded eagerly, all thoughts of playing it cool, taking it slow, abandoned. I watched him walk away, committed his every step to memory, until he was out of sight.

I was smitten.

Chapter Two

My faithful little car got me home as swiftly as
safe driving would allow. I was online and typing
plans for our next date before the kettle had boiled.
He responded at once: neither of us was in the mood
for playing games. We liked each other-a lot! Why
waste time?

Slow down…you don't know this man. Not really.

An unwelcome, intrusive thought. I pushed it
away, chose instead to put my trust in giddy emotion.
Sensible caution must not be permitted to spoil this
new adventure or dilute the delicious taste of surging
excitement.

We decided against another date in town, choosing
instead to enjoy the cosy intimacy of my pretty little
cottage.

Too soon, too soon. He's a stranger…

He arranged an early train, so as to give us as long
a day together as possible . I would pick him up from
the station on Saturday morning. Five days to wait.
Five long days!

At last, the day arrived. I'd chosen my outfit days
before- dusted off the iron, smoothed stubborn
wardrobe wrinkles into submission- so had plenty of
time to style my hair. Half a head into the process of
blow drying a bouncy curl, disaster struck. Power cut!

I cursed and raged against my terrible luck. Cried bitter tears of disappointment. The romantic meal I'd planned would not make it to the table. I'd have to cancel. But…he'd think I didn't like him after all. See it as a brush-off. I was going to make this work, dammit! This was my life, maybe even my future. *Our* future…I was in a daze of romantic fantasy. A simple power cut couldn't be permitted to dim that daze. I gnawed at my lower lip, plotting. I had a drawerful of candles and the local chippy was a five-minute drive away. Problem solved! Fish and chip supper by candlelight. Perfect! I brightened, immediately cheered, before catching sight of my half blow-dried hair in the mirror. Shit!

A couple of hours later I was parking my car by the station, marching towards the sliding doors, making my way to the waiting room. Vigorous toweling had left me with attractively (I hoped) tousled hair. Our Clock told me I was ten minutes early. Perfect. The metal chair was far less uncomfortable than I remembered. Perching happily, pulsing with anticipation, I turned my eyes towards the railway track

His train pulled in. My stomach played host to a swarm of excited butterflies as they performed a spirited group flamenco. Our long week's wait was almost over- we were about to be reunited!

11

He wasn't on the train. The butterflies turned to stone and fell into the pit of my stomach. Disappointment swelled behind my eyes and overflowed as hot tears. With a deep, shuddering breath I fished my phone from my handbag. One '*thanks for nothing*' text, then I'd block.

A message. *Sorry, missed train. Will be on next one. X*

In the end, it wasn't the next train, but the one after that. Two unexpected hours sitting in increasing discomfort wasn't exactly part of my plan for the day, but he would be worth the wait. Besides, it gave me a chance to catch up on my trashy mag reading. I browsed the magazine stand outside the little newsagents and chose the one with the most screamingly lurid headlines. I was in the mood for pure escapism. Engrossed in '*Lying Hubby Had a SECRET WIFE for 17 YEARS-Shock Way I Found Out*' I didn't notice train number three pull in. Consequently, I missed his approach; he caught me devouring junk journalism, a liberal sprinkling of crisp crumbs decorating my décolletage.

"Tittle-Tattle? You read that stuff?" He raised an eyebrow "You *sure* you're a Librarian?!

Too late I remembered the battered Bukowski I'd left in the car-why hadn't I let him catch me reading that? I gave an easy laugh."Oh, you've got to read some trash occasionally, you know? Makes you really appreciate the great writing!"

He smiled, made a "fair point well made" face and offered me his arm.

"Shall we? Can't wait to see your cottage-sounds lovely!"

And lovely it was. Kitchy vintage was definitely my thing. As we stepped into the living room , I crossed my fingers, hoping he'd be impressed by my maximalist interior design. He paused, taking it all in.

Above the log burner, a mantelpiece played host to a riot of spaghetti poodles, ceramic flamingoes and plastic Babycham deer. Higher on the wall Tretchikoff's "Green Lady" regarded the room with downcast eyes. A hideous piece of Murano glass squatted in the centre of my painted wooden dining table, into which were thrust purple hydrangea pom-poms , hastily torn from the garden that morning. On each side of the squidgy sofa (my only modern piece) matching Ercol side tables stood to attention, also crammed with decorative doodahs.

He gave a low whistle.

"You weren't joking when you said you loved a good rummage around a charity shop were you?"

I bristled slightly, then forced a smile.

"I do, but I'd be lucky to find some of these pieces at a charity shop. See her?" I gestured towards my

bookcase, on which was displayed a bust of Marilyn
Monroe. "Won at auction. Had to bid like a demon to
win her" I gave a sheepish grin "Caught a bit of
auction fever and went waaay above my limit. But
£300 later and she was mine forever." I gave the bust
a playful tap on the nose. "And I love her."

He drew me towards him "Surrounding yourself
with things you love….so important." his voice
dropped to a low murmur "so very….very…
important" punctuating each word with a soft kiss on
my neck , working up to my lips.

Driving to pick up a chippy tea was now out of the
question. Giddy with anticipation, I scampered up the
steep wooden uncarpeted stairs, him following
closely behind. The pounding of my excited heart
matched the thudding of our feet. He excused himself
while I lit candles. Flickering flame sent shadows
reaching across the bedroom, exploring plump
feather pillows,eiderdown,and elegant brass bedstead.
Carefully polished metal reflected the candlelight:
shards of light moving like fireflies in their mating
dance of seduction. I'd chosen vanilla-scented
candles. The air grew heavy with notes of chocolate,
caramel, and cream. I arranged myself on the bed -
legs stretched seductively, arms above my head wrists
up, my smile slow, sexy…I waited.

Silence. Then the soft padding of footsteps. With a

low creak, the door opened. My heart fluttered like never before. Well, not since that day I spotted an original chalkware lamp in the window of Help the Aged anyway. In he came.

He was still fully clothed. The only change was that he now wore a wooly beanie hat instead of grandad's trilby. Uncomfortable to sleep in, surely? My brow puckered, puzzled…then I sniggered.

"It's not that cold Mr! Heating off in June isn't a problem-you should try it here in January- proper chilly! Here." I reached out for him "Pop that thing off and let me warm you up…" I ratcheted up the sexy smile by couple of notches.

My laughter was not reciprocated. Due to the limited light, I couldn't clearly read his expression, but I thought I saw his jaw tighten. My smile dropped.

"The hat stays."

He lay down next to me. Not touching. Not speaking.

I watched his face in profile. His brows were low, his lips- so recently dancing enticingly around my throat- set in a cold, hard line.

"The hat stays" he repeated. "OK?"

The '*OK*' wasn't an '*are you OK with that?*' It was a firm '*This is not up for discussion. Ever.*'

We lay in silence, the warmth of our recent

15

embraces entirely absent. Listening as his breathing fell into a slow, heavy rhythm, I replayed the evening over in my head. Tried to work out what I'd done wrong.

I whispered, "are you awake?"

No reply. Just the deep, regular breath of sleep. Eventually, I slept too.

Over time, the importance of the hat became clear. He was losing his hair-something else I was yet to discover-but it wasn't about trivial vanity. The more hair he lost, the more he noticed how closely he resembled his father. Hatless, he couldn't bear to look at himself. Or be looked at.

I awoke wrapped tightly in the comforting warmth of his arms. It hadn't been the evening I had hoped for, but this was…nice. Very nice.

I lifted my head off his chest to study his sleeping face. Long dark lashes trembled as he slumbered. His lips curled in a gentle smile as an indecipherable mutter escaped. He looked peaceful. Happy. My heart swelled with the warmth of contentment. A fierce need to protect him took hold.

We spent the morning ambling around my village. He was a city boy, had never spent much time in the countryside, and was enchanted by the peace of rural living. His obvious enjoyment made me happy. I was flattered that he loved the place I'd chosen to make my home.

In the afternoon, we headed for the village pub. He was delighted to discover a pool table - racked up and chalked a cue whilst I fetched two pints of icy-cold pear cider. I was a terrible player. We laughed together at my hopeless attempts to pot a ball. He played with consummate skill and tried to show me how it was done. As the afternoon drew to a close, I was finally able to sink one ball into a pocket- one that I had actually aimed for! He celebrated my success with applause and kisses.

All too soon, it was time for him to leave. I drove him to the station where we said our goodbyes under Our Clock. The hug he gave me was uncomfortably tight. Eventually, I came up for air, only to be crushed back into his chest again.

He leaned down, putting his lips close to my ear. I heard a barely audible whisper- *I love you* - before being abruptly released. Turning on his heel, without a backwards glance, he strode towards the sliding doors and disappeared into the crowd.

I didn't leave immediately. I stood perfectly still, under the clock. Watching its hands measure the time since he left. Trying to untangle the bundle of emotions I was feeling. I pulled at one thread- overwhelming happiness. Another thread- confusion. Yet another- a sense of trepidation, of fear. I

17

discarded that particular thread, bunched it back into the bundle, and pulled again at the thread of happiness. That was the one I wanted.

Over the next few weeks, Saturday became our day. We explored the area, visited all the places I knew so well. I'd grown up in the next village along and I adored it. Of course, I'd lived in other places, but this had always been my home. Wherever I was, I always knew I'd head back here one day. It had everything, right on the doorstep: little shop, doctor's surgery, a beautiful river to wander by, village pub. Every Christmas a tree loaded with coloured lights would appear on the village green. From my bedroom window, I would watch and listen as the local choir belted out Christmas carols from under the tree on Boxing Day. There was a sense of community here. Neighbours would take it in turns visiting elderly residents. Community events regularly took place at the ancient village hall: morning yoga sessions, theatrical performances, peaceful book group meetings and chaotic children's parties. The local schools were staffed by teachers who had taught generations of the same families. Children grew to adults here and stayed to raise their own families. It was a safe place. A happy place.

He was charmingly excited to see into my life -the river I'd swum in as a child, the little cafe where I'd had my first real job, the quaint old sweet shop where I'd spent my pocket money after school many years ago. I loved sharing all these things with him, drawing him into my world. Seen through his eyes, my upbringing seemed idyllic. I suppose it was…I had never really given it much thought or considered my good fortune in being born into a family who loved me and cared for me in a place of beauty and peace.

During those first weeks, he told me very little about his own childhood, preferring to talk about mine. I was flattered by his interest, never stopping to consider how much he was learning about me and how little I'd learned about him. I knew the basics- that he was the youngest of four, with three older sisters, and had a stepdad who he seemed fond of. His parents had divorced when he was around seven and he'd been brought up in Leeds.

When he *did* share happy memories, they were of his grandfather. He'd spent hours in grandad's immaculate garden, pulling weeds and hunting for the tiny stone frog that mysteriously moved to a new spot each
week.

Beyond that, he shared very little. I didn't care. It was the person he was today I was most interested in, not who he had been.

He was far more forthcoming about what interested him: his great love of music and poetry. He would recite his favourite poems-works by Pablo Naruda, Sara Teasdale,Khalil Gibran. His diversions were solitary ones-things he could submerge himself in, connecting only to the artist. I was flattered that he had chosen me to share his passions with-that he instinctively knew I would understand.

One thing disturbed the tranquility of our Saturdays-his guilt over leaving the cat to fend for herself for an entire evening. I suggested he brought her with him for our next weekend. She hated her travel box and fought him with the ferocity of a miniature tiger when he put her inside- he had the scratches to prove it! Once she was at my house, it made perfect sense for her to stay with me while he travelled to and fro. I'd been petless since losing my dog a couple of years earlier- a devastating loss that only another bereaved pet owner could possibly understand- so I was happy to welcome her into my home. She meant a great deal to him, describing her as his 'support animal'- said she was actually registered as such, which was why his landlord had made an exception to the No Pets rule.

Once Cleocatra (yes, really!) was happily settled, there was really no need for us to endure the recurring pain of 'weekend end' goodbyes. His work as a freelance writer meant he could relocate easily. And quickly.

We never discussed living together, but it happened anyway.

Six short weeks after our first date, we were sharing a home.

I was blissfully happy.

Chapter Three

He'd say our life was a happy bubble, just the two of us. Together. Us against the world. Safe.

I loved it too, that happy little bubble, but there were other people I cared about, and I was keen for him to meet them. Extend our social circle, but carefully- he was shy around strangers. I gave it some thought, then picked up the phone.   Dan and Carol were two of my oldest and dearest friends. Well, at least Carol was. We'd met, pre-Dan, at a family wedding. Probably 20 years ago, maybe more. Her joyfully uncoordinated moves during the inevitable evening disco had drawn me to her. I'd watched with a mix of envy and admiration – oh, to be that unselfconscious! My awkward shuffling on the dance floor had brought me into her orbit. I was seized, spun and shimmied with without so much as a formal introduction. She'd shown me how to pull off her signature moves: the mashed potato, watusi, swim and twist. Finally, we shook our last tail feather and headed for the free bar, where we remained in animated conversation until the cocktails ran dry. We'd been staunch friends ever since. Proudly independent and happily single, I was a little surprised when she told me all about the fabulous new man she'd met. Surprised and a little jealous. The'd fallen into happy coupledom almost instantly. It was so obviously a meeting of soulmates-Dan made her deliriously happy. Impossible not to feel delighted for them. He was as outgoing and kind as she. They'd set up home together with fearless haste and had played host to some of the best party nights of my life. Both were talented artists - painters. I'd sat for them a couple of times in the cosy art studio they'd created within their rambling converted barn. A menagerie of rescued creatures shared their home: goats, pigs, chickens, a solitary cow, bad tempered donkey and a couple of geese. Both were warm and generous hosts- I was certain they would put him at his ease.

It took all my powers of persuasion, but eventually he agreed to a visit.

"You'll love them" I reassured him. "They are the loveliest people I know."

The barn stood in splendid isolation. An ancient valley, formed in the far distant past by the combined powers of gravity, water and ice. sheltered the building with its steeply rising sides. The drive over was glorious. I'd got hold of one of his favourite albums by The Velvet Underground. Skimming through the countryside, we sang our hearts out. He had a good voice, belting out a passible Lou Reed vocal: much more tuneful than my attempt to imitate Nico's stentorian drawl. He roared with laughter at my rendition of 'I'll Be Your Mirror.' With a heavy accent I overemphasised every syllable, willing him to really listen and believe that I meant those words for him. Happy, relaxed and comforted, he gazed at the passing scenery: a riot of lush, verdant green. Bursting with life. Pleasing to the eye and soothing to the soul.

Closely crowded trees conspired to hide Carol's home from the rest of the world, but I'd taken this trip many times before - even the challenging criss-cross of deeply pitted country lanes couldn't delay us. We arrived ahead of time before Dan had managed to corral the geese and were greeted by a barrage of honking and hissing. Dan appeared, sprinting as fast as humanly possible whilst hampered by oversized wellies and two excited trip hazard terriers.

"Mabel! Doris!" he roared "Guests, not intruders! *Guests!*"

He managed to shoo the geese through a nearby gate into a field of overgrown grass. They were clearly taking their guard duties seriously. Lingering by the sagging five bar gate and straining their sinewy necks suspiciously, they kept us under close observation with an unblinking orange-yellow gaze.

"Sorry about that-better than guard dogs, geese! Come in, come in! Carol's just slaughtered one of our best ducks for lunch-you can help with the plucking!"

"It's OK" I whispered, "he's joking. They're vegan."

Carol greeted us at the door, wild salt-and-pepper

hair skewered into submission by what looked like a knitting needle, a light dusting of flour liberally coating her tangerine kaftan.

"Come here beautiful girl!" She commanded "It's been an age!"

Before I could protest, I found myself seized and enveloped by her comfortably fleshy arms. Confronted by joyously unrestrained bosoms, I managed to draw in a lungful of air before my access to oxygen was momentarily blocked.

"And is this the gorgeous man we've heard so little about?" A gentle rebuke-I had been a very bad friend lately. "Come here this instant!"

He was engulfed in an enthusiastic embrace, similar to the one from which I had just been released. Fortunately, his towering height meant he was not at risk of suffocation.Carol, generous hostess that she was, had gone to a great deal of effort over lunch. We sat down to liberal helpings of vegetable quiche, arugula salad dressed with lemon vinaigrette, wholemeal scones and homemade jams.

He was a little reserved, but Dan and Carol were a lot to take in and so intensely garrulous that I hardly got a word in myself! They were infectiously jovial. I knew without checking that he would be enjoying himself and resolved to arrange more outings for the four of us.

Conversation flowed: books, theatre, village gossip, politics, memories of the past and plans for the future. Their passion for art was evidenced by eclectic decor: furniture painted in exuberant hues of blue, orange and yellow, clay masks hanging haphazardly from whitewashed walls, a hatstand groaning beneath the weight of flamboyant hats and scarves. On every surface, jam jars crammed with wildflowers surrounded sculpted figures, looking for all the world like strange alien beings exploring a landscape dominated by gigantic blooms.

After lunch, a walk to meet the animals was proposed. Our unsuitable footwear was examined and pronounced unfit for purpose. After a quick rummage under the stairs, spare wellies were unearthed.

Watching Dan surreptitiously tip what appeared to be several dead spiders out of the proffered Hunters, he was reluctant to try them on, but after some encouragement slipped them on gingerly.

The yard was a sea of semi-liquid mud. Treacherously slippy underfoot.

"Glad of those wellies now I bet!" Dan slapped him on the back. "Just imagine what this would have done to your fancy trainers!"

He gave a weak smile that didn't quite reach his eyes.

Dan and Carol's well looked after pack of rescued animals were in lively spirits. A brood of sparsely feathered hens pecked eagerly at handfuls of scattered feed. Each was sporting a miniature woollen vest, knitted in poorly matched shades of clashing colour.

"Ex battery hens" explained Carol. "Hardly any feathers because of the way they were kept." she shook her head sadly "No space to move, no natural light, stuck in their own droppings...poor girls. So, we get these vests made for them."

28

"Will they have to dress like that for ever?"

Dan chortled "Only if they're very lucky! I'm having one knitted in my size-can't wait to pop it on."

Carol ignored him "No, not for ever. Only until their feathers grow in. It'll take a while, but they'll get there-won't you, my pretty girls?"

With a sad little smile, she gave the nearest hen an affectionate pat. It flinched, quickly moving out of reach before resuming its peck and scratch routine. We were introduced to Pepper the donkey - *not too close- she's a kicker!* - nibbled by a collection of playful goats and honked at again by the ever-vigilant geese.

As we approached the pigsty, I saw his face brighten. Hurrying over to lean in, he reached out and scratched its enormous inhabitant behind one fleshy ear. He was rewarded with a high-pitched squeal.

"Ah, that's Squealer! Isn't he beautiful?" Dan leant over and joined in the scratching. "You've made a friend for life there-he only squeals like that for the good guys! Don't you, my little mate?"

29

The 'little mate', easily 4 foot tall at the shoulder, groaned in ecstasy and manoeuvred his great bulk closer to the fence.

Carol gave me a swift wink that said, '*well played girl-he's quite the catch!*'

I winked back. Yes, he certainly was.

We had to leave before it got too dark to navigate the maze of potholes that served as roads. I gave our thanks and farewells and received yet more warm hugs from Carol and a box of fruit and vegetables from Dan.

"Great to see you both!" Dan yelled over the sound of the car engine "We've got a wassail in the orchard planned - all the locals will be there - you should come along!"

I nodded and grinned, giving a cheery thumbs up as we made our way carefully down the lane.

On the drive home, he was quiet, subdued. Seemed deep in thought. Probably overwhelmed by our recent overdose of bonhomie. I filled the silence with happy chatter, marvelling over Carol's banjo skills and

Dan's relentless ebullience.

"He's a riot, that one! Did you hear what he said about the geese and that bag of frozen peas? How did they even…."

"He's an arsehole." He spoke without looking at me- his voice flat, expressionless.

I was puzzled "You didn't like him?"

"Like him? LIKE HIM??! What's to FUCKING LIKE?? He was all over you for FUCKS SAKE! Right in front of me AND his missus. I mean, Jesus Christ! Did you like it, him drooling all over you like a sex-starved dog? You weren't exactly pushing him away, were you? How the fuck do you think that made me feel??"

A shockingly sudden explosion of intense rage. At full volume, in the confines of my little car, his voice instantly filled me with fear. I felt the colour drain from my face. Shocked tears spilled silently and rolled fatly down my cheeks.

"How fucking humiliating! How DARE you put me in a position like that!!! Why didn't you tell him to FUCK RIGHT OFF!!??? Have you fucked him before??? Is that why you took me there, so you could rub my face in it, you absolute BITCH???!!!"

And so, it continued, only stopping when we arrived at my cottage. I wept all the way. Oblivious to my distress, his roaring had left him breathless and exhausted.

I felt numb. He slammed his way into my home. Took the stairs two at a time, kicked open the bedroom door, threw himself onto the bed.

Standing in the lounge, I tried to process what had just happened. *Had* Dan been flirting with me? Replaying his every word and gesture, I tried to see what he'd seen. What had I missed? I'd always been naive when it came to men, had more than once misinterpreted flirtation as polite interest. It had landed me in hot water before.

Then with a jolt, I remembered the affair that Dan had confessed to a few years back. A silly, meaningless fling that had nevertheless hurt Carol deeply. It had looked like the end for a while, but they travelled together through a long, painful journey of repair, at the end of which they managed to find each other again.

Oh God. What a humiliating position for me to put him in!

I listened at the foot of the stairs. Silence…I strained my ears, trying to block out the sound of my pounding blood. Could I hear him crying? Treading softly, I crept up the stairs. Gently opened the bedroom door.

He lay with his face turned to the wall; knees drawn up towards his chest. With the curtains drawn it was difficult to be sure, but I thought I saw his shoulders shuddering.

Slowly and carefully, I joined him on the bed. Slipped my arm around him and found his hand. Gave it a sympathetic squeeze. Held my breath. For a second or two, he gave no response. Then, I felt him grip my hand. Relief flooded through me. I held him until, exhausted by emotion, we both slept.

Chapter Four

Sleeping- or at least lying beside me- was one of the
few things that calmed him. Increasingly dependent
on my physical presence, he would suffer panic
attacks through the hours I was not able to be with
him. I only ever left him to go to work; was doing all
I could to be by his side as much as possible. After
our disastrous visit to Dan and Carol's, I dropped all
plans to introduce him to friends and family. I
couldn't risk putting him in a situation that might
cause him pain ever again. My own behaviour could
be modified. Over time, I learned what to say and
what not to say: how to act, move, *be*. There was no
way I could expect others to show him the same
consideration. A throwaway comment, a facial
expression, a joke or a gesture - all could be
misinterpreted by him as deliberate attempts to
undermine or ridicule. His self-esteem was so fragile,
so easily wounded, that he constantly saw bad intent
in the words or actions of others. Gradually, he gave
up all the things that meant he'd have to leave the
house. I was particularly sad to see him abandon his
voluntary work. It had been good for him to think
about the needs of others and to actively try to help. I
felt it gave him a healthy distraction from self-
absorption - although of course I never voiced that

34

opinion. My workplace was in a small town, about half an hour's drive away. I'd noticed several charity shops on the high street. Wouldn't it be great, I'd said, if you volunteered at one of those shops? I could drop you on the way to work and pick you up on my way home. You wouldn't be alone all day *and* could spend more time with me. Keep me company during my drives to and fro. He'd received the suggestion in silence, before becoming agitated:

"Jesus Christ! I can just imagine your fucking jealousy if I had to work with women. What if a pretty girl came in? You'd flip your fucking lid! No way am I putting myself through that shit-your fucking possessive bollocks! I can't even LOOK at a woman without you going mental. Fucking crazy bitch..."

He continued to berate me until late into the night. Rising in volume until he was in a state of screaming hysteria. Protestations cut no ice at all. In fact, they prolonged the ordeal.

Honestly, I couldn't recall ever acting in the ways he was describing. Was I unconsciously reacting with jealousy if he mentioned another woman? Perhaps he was reading those feelings in my expression – he was extremely sensitive. I promised myself I'd be more careful in future.

Each evening after work, he would be waiting for

me: cup of tea in hand, at the same time every day. If I were delayed by more than a few minutes, he'd become terribly anxious. I'd hear the pinging of messages as I parked the car: *where are you? Are you ok? Are you working late?* a continuous stream of texts, fired off with no pause to allow for a response. Indoors, he'd be wild-eyed and terrified, occasionally tearful. Or worse-furious and screaming. I'd need to lie next to him almost immediately until his breathing slowed, and he was able to relax.

Because he needed me to lie still and silent, this increasingly regular routine left me exhausted. If I moved in my sleep, he would wake me up immediately- screaming, sobbing, hitting himself or lifting my eyelids with his fingers. He'd use the piercingly bright light from his phone so he could '*see my beautiful eyes looking back at him.*' Lying in one position for hour after hour became painful. Parts of my body felt bruised. I worried about developing bedsores. He said he felt more alone if I slept -almost as if I had left him, abandoned him in favour of spending my time somewhere he couldn't follow. He would sleep during the day, so that he could spend the night with me. Awake. Making the most of our time together. Consequently, I was unable to snatch more than an hour or so. He rarely slept - not while I was at home anyway. My working days were busy. I had to be 'on the go' from 7am until 5pm, then drive for half an hour to get home. I struggled with exhaustion, suffered with frequent migraines and bouts of dizziness.

He developed night terrors: screaming, sobbing, gasping for air. It was traumatic listening to him. Traumatic and terrifying. Perhaps 'night terrors' isn't correct, as they happen while the victim is asleep. And he was awake. All I know is that I would be jolted into consciousness by the sounds of his distress. Loud, insistent, frightening. He would even lash out with a kick or slap, apologising tearfully when he accidentally hurt me.

I could see he was in terrible pain and wanted desperately to comfort him. Heal him. Somebody or something had hurt him badly.

Finally, he told me what had destroyed his peace of mind. Then it all made sense.

Chapter Five

He was three the first time his father sexually assaulted him. It happened in his bedroom. The smallest bedroom in the house, crowded with toys typically gifted to little boys: robots, cars, plastic dinosaurs. Afraid of the dark, he'd slept under the soft glow of his nightlight –a round plastic representation of the full moon. The perfect room for a little boy to sleep in. A place where he should have been safe from harm. Up until that point, he *had* been safe but that night, while his mother slept, his father took that away forever.

After he took me into his confidence, he spoke about the abuse every single day. It consumed him, the horror of it. I cried with him, held him for hours while he sobbed, cradled in my arms. The things he told me were shocking; monstrous. Things that I couldn't have survived as an adult, yet he'd suffered all that as a helpless, innocent child. At the hands of a man who should have been his protector. A terrible betrayal. Beyond evil. The suffering he went through haunted me — still does to this day.

He'd sob himself into a frenzy. Scream at his father as if he was in the room with us. Cry out for his mother to wake up, come for him, *do* something. Night after night. The only thing that soothed him was holding me close. I lay without moving and listened. He had perfect recall of every time his father abused him. The nights he lay awake, paralyzed and helpless, waiting for the soft sound of his bedroom door sliding open. Every time he was shared with other pedophiles. The Wednesday after school football sessions that he'd struggle through, knowing his father would collect him when the last whistle blew and drive him to a house where a group of men would be waiting. How his father would hand him over *'he's a good boy. He knows what to do…'* The photos that were taken, that he imagined being shared online still. Thinking about these nameless, faceless monsters getting sick enjoyment from mementoes of his child body undergoing unspeakable tortures…he would howl with rage and pain.

It was unbelievably hard to listen without being physically sick. Of course, I'd always felt revulsion by the thought of such abhorrent crimes - found it hard to sit through news reports outlining similar cases - but I'd never been this close to someone who'd suffered such violations. Here in front of me was a man who had been effectively destroyed before his life had properly begun. It was a form of murder: the man he might have been was lost the moment his father began to use his tiny body for his own satisfaction. I don't have the words to adequately express how disgusted I was at the thought of... It was hideous. Utterly repugnant. He too struggled to articulate his feelings. Instead, he expressed himself with cries of grief, rage, pain: animalistic sounds. The sounds of a soul being ripped apart, of a mind disintegrating under the unbearable weight of unspeakable memories.

I was desperate to help him. I would try to love him better. Give him everything he needed from me, so he could find some peace. But I felt totally overwhelmed and helpless. I wasn't equipped for this. I didn't have the skills or the knowledge to fix him, no matter how much I wanted to. We needed to get him proper support. Somebody with expert knowledge of how a broken mind could be healed. I suggested making an appointment with my doctor as a starting point. Secretly, I felt that he needed to be hospitalised and hoped that a visit to my GP would put wheels in motion, but any talk of visiting a doctor was quickly and angrily shut down. *I've tried that* he told me. *It didn't help. Nothing ever will.* He'd got angry and I learned not to make that suggestion again.

He told me he'd made several attempts at suicide; described in detail which methods he'd tried, why he'd failed. Fascinated by celebrities who had taken their own lives, he would talk about them with something that sounded like admiration or envy. As if he wished he had been as successful as they. I spent my days at work terrified of what I might find when I got home.

Once, I suggested we report his father to the police. Wouldn't that help him? Bring it all out into daylight so it was no longer a secret, lurking in the shadows? Seeing his father punished for what he did - wouldn't that make him feel more in control? He was horrified at the suggestion: furious that I'd even suggested it. Did I think he could face reporting his father? Potentially have to be in the same room as him? Was I *really* that fucking stupid?

I tried to distract him from constantly replaying each horrific crime committed against his infant self. Sometimes, it worked for a while. We talked - even laughed -as I shared my own life with him. I'd had a wonderful childhood-supportive and loving parents, a happy home, everything a child deserves and needs to grow into a happy, healthy adult. He listened to my memories of a childhood he should have had, one that every child deserves. Filled with love.

Sometimes he could be persuaded to sit in the garden with me, but only in the middle of the night when it would be just us. No neighbours in their gardens, no passersby that might stop to chat. Just us and the darkness. He would be calm then. The rage would ebb away for a short time. He'd watch the

41

nighttime sky and share the few happy memories that he had. Most were about his grandfather; the one adult he felt had loved him. He'd tell me we all contained energy that would be released back into the universe at the moment of our death. When he died, the pure energy that had been his grandfather would find him. Join with him into one beautiful piece of light and love. He would be with his grandfather forever, travelling the universe. *That'll be us now though,* he'd say, *you and me, together. One piece of energy, forever. Free.* I had no belief in any sort of afterlife, but I smiled and supported his belief, tracing the stars and imagining the worlds we'd visit as our spirits mingled with whatever was up there. It came to be his only hope for a happy future. Our afterlife.

Chapter Six

One night, safely cocooned in our bed, at his instigation we shared our experiences of past relationships. His had been few and far between. His first girlfriend, back when he was a teenager, had been instrumental in him losing his home.

She had been a horrified witness to a violent attack by his stepfather. Apparently, it wasn't just his biological father who had been abusive. His mother's second husband had come into his life when he was just seven years old and had disciplined him with utter cruelty. He was beaten. Locked in cupboards for hours. Had his teeth ripped out with a pair of plyers...*Hard to believe nobody noticed. Surely that would have left obvious wounds?* Whilst trapped in the suffocating darkness of the single wardrobe in his sister's room, he had comforted himself with a battered Walkman: earphones clamped tightly over his small ears. I began to understand his passionate love for singers and their songs. As a child, music had been both a comfort and a distraction - an escape from horrors. As an adult, it was a way relate to the experiences of others and to feel less alone in his suffering.

He felt deep connection with musicians who sang of their own pain. "Anger Rising" by Jerry Cantrell,

"Disarm" by The Smashing Pumpkins,"Candyman" by Siouxsie and the Banshees were all on his playlist. He had an encyclopedic knowledge of songs that dealt with the horror of abuse. A comfort to him, quite disturbing for me. The realisation that such abhorrent violation of childhood was common enough to be explored by so many musicians was something that appalled me.

Strangely, he spoke fondly of his stepfather: '*he didn't know any better. He'd had a bad time too.*' Sometimes, during one of his hysterical breakdowns, he'd cry out for his stepdad to come for him. He was a 'better' father than the man who had helped create him because his assaults had never been sexual. The attack his teenaged girlfriend had witnessed prompted her to contact the police. They had investigated. Visited his family home, questioned the adults in the house but asked him nothing at all. His mother sided with her husband; '*Just a family argument. Boys will be boys.*' No action was taken. After this incident he was ordered from the house. Seventeen and homeless. Another betrayal.

So, what about you?" He asked. "How many boyfriends?"

A rare chance to talk about my life instead of his. I decided to keep it light, perhaps divert him from the misery of his own youthful experiences.

"Oh, you know-more than ten, less than twenty? Not worth keeping a tally!"

I was trying to tell him nobody before him had meant enough to me to even be worth remembering. Trying to be flippant. That was not how he interpreted my words.

He paused; half smiled. Lay in silence for a moment or two. I heard him mutter *'naughty girl'* and something about making us a cup of tea.

I listened to him go downstairs. Fill the kettle. Then silence. Minutes went by. Then half an hour. I strained my ears against the hush of night. I wasn't supposed to leave the bedroom unless he was with me, but I was worried. He needed me. I made my mind up to go and find him.

I found him in the garden, sitting on our bench. A cigarette dangling between his fingers, an inch of ash clinging precariously to the stub. His face expressionless.

I sat beside him and silently took his hand. He did not return my squeeze, his hand limp in mine. Minutes passed.

"You fat old slag" he murmured.

For a moment, I thought I'd misheard him, until he turned to face me. His expression was twisted with hate. He looked disgusted: scowled and curled his upper lip, bared his teeth. From his throat came a chilling, animalistic sound- somewhere between a growl and a hiss. I froze. Shifted from watchful and wary to terrified in an instant.

Releasing his hand, I stood up carefully. Retreated inside, hoping time alone would return him to the gentle man I loved.

I heard the door slam thunderously.

He caught up with me at the top of the stairs. Grabbed each of my wrists. Hard. Backed me against a wall and moved forward until our foreheads rested together. Slowly, he lifted his head from mine then brought it back, connecting. A small headbutt. He continued pushing until my head was trapped between his and the wall behind me. His eyes blazed into mine. I had never felt so hated. Or so frightened. Accurately reading the emotions behind my expression, his eyes blazed with fresh fury.

"You think I would hurt you?? You think I'm like my father? I can hold it in better than him! Stand there!"

He gestured, indicating the spot. I was released from his grip but still couldn't move. Completely paralysed. I couldn't speak. I think I may have whimpered.

"I SAID STAND THERE!!"

The ferocity of his words galvanised me into movement. I obeyed, standing with my back to the staircase. He moved in front of me. Stood close, forcing me to lean back a little. Ordered me to stay still.

The drop behind me-uncarpeted, steep, hard - frightened me. What was in front of me frightened me even more. I waited obediently. Trying to keep my expression passive. Eyeing me carefully, he took a couple of steps back. Made a fist with his right hand and punched at the air next to my head. Again, and again. I felt the air move violently with each punch and fought to keep my eyes open. All the while he was screaming a barely coherent string of obscenities.

I suppose he was showing me his self-restraint. He wanted badly to hurt me, but he wouldn't. He could stop himself, fight against his instincts. He was a Good Man.

At last, it stopped. Without a word, he turned away from me and went back into the bedroom. I heard the bed springs creak as he settled himself.

I quietly took a cautious few steps away from my precarious position. Released the breath I'd been holding on to and waited. No sound from the bedroom. Minutes passed.

I should have run from the house. I didn't. Instead, I went back into the bedroom. Slowly got into bed. Laid down next to him.Squeezed my eyes closed tight. I realised I'd wet myself. Too afraid to get up to clean myself, I prayed he wouldn't notice.

Chapter Seven

Getting up the next day was not easy. I inched myself off the bed slowly, padded out of the room as quietly as I was able. My body felt bruised - *had he injured me?* In the shower, I checked myself carefully for signs of damage. Nothing. Yet I was in pain-my skin felt tender; my muscles ached. *What was this- flu? Was I ill?* Eyes burning with exhaustion and unspilled tears, I gingerly toweled myself dry. The steel trap of an approaching migraine tightened its grip. I splashed cold water, took a couple of pain killers and prayed it wouldn't incapacitate me.

Unusually, he was out of bed and in the kitchen. As I entered, he held out a cup of tea in a cleanish mug. Accepting it cautiously, I offered him a weak smile of thanks.

"I feel really bad today. Really, really bad. Ring in sick Love. Please? I need you."

To buy myself a little time before answering, I took a long sip of tea. I was going to go to work. Just as I did every day. Work was where I felt safe, where I took refuge in normalcy. And I was frightened- had to get away from him for a few hours. Eyeing the distance between us and the front door, I weighed up my chances of getting outside before he did. No chance at all. Here goes. I feigned a look of sorrowful regret.

"I'm sorry Love, but we've got a lot on today. I really need to be at work. Sorry."

I held my breath.

There was a small flash of irritation in his eyes, quickly replaced by a look of sorrowful dejection.

"OK Love." Spoken quietly, resignedly. "I'll try. I love you" the last words spoken in a halting whisper, heartbreakingly vulnerable.

He took the cup from my unresisting hand and drew me to him. Held me tightly. I flinched a little but relaxed into the embrace before he noticed. We stood there for a few minutes, swaying gently. I put my arms around him and rocked him in a gentle rhythm. When I felt it was safe to do so, I extricated myself.

"Sorry Love, I have to go. I'm going to be late."

No objections from him, just a sigh, a drop of the shoulders and a look of quiet resignation.
His eyes followed me as I left.

I arrived at work with no recollection of the drive at all. Spent the day on autopilot: managed all the challenges and interactions of the day with no indication that I was struggling. Engaged in cheerful chit chat with colleagues with the expected smiles and laughter. I dreaded the inevitable day when somebody would notice and ask all those questions I was so afraid of: *are you ok? Can I help? Why don't you just leave?* I was colluding with him, keeping our secret. The thought of others *knowing...* shameful, And disloyal.

All too soon, the working day was over, and I was parking my car in the driveway. Feeling the familiar tension rise. I paused. Impossible to prepare myself when I had no idea what I was about to walk into. Would he be angry that I'd gone to work and abandoned him? Had he spent the day stewing with resentment? Was I safe? What if he'd...was *he* safe? What was I *thinking*? He needed me!

I hurried into the house. Called out his name. Silence. Maybe he was in bed? No. Where was he? Had he left me? A small flame of hope flickered, quickly extinguished by a wave of guilt.

I found him in the spare bedroom. He was kneeling next to the wardrobe, a twisted sheet wrapped around the handle, the other end tightly wound around his neck. His face a mess of snot and tears.

A terrifying, heart-rending scene. One that I knew with chilly certainty had been manufactured. He had arranged himself in that way. I knew it. It was too well timed, too manufactured, too perfectly posed to cause maximum shock and distress.

Looking back at that moment, I've berated myself

a million times for not calling his bluff. I should have reached out for help, picked up the phone: ambulance, police, *someone*. He could have been sectioned for his own safety, under the care of a mental health team. And I would have been safe from him. *He* would have been safe from him. But I was still absurdly loyal, wanting to do what I thought would give the most comfort. This was a cry for sympathy and support. I gave him what he needed.

Running to him, I knelt beside him. wrapped myself around him. We cried together until exhaustion took over and we slept, right there on the floor, a tangle of limbs, so close that it was hard to know where he ended, and I began. I slept like the dead. Woke in pain, yet curiously numb.

It was another working day. He didn't press me to stay home. He didn't speak at all, just watched me as I prepared to leave. No pleas, threats or demands. Nothing. I found his silence unnerving but held onto my cheerful demeanor.

"I'll be home soon Love. As soon as I can."

He nodded. Expressionless. Did not return my goodbye kiss.

My day followed the increasingly familiar pattern: stitched on smiles and a headful of troubled thoughts. The respite of work was becoming less and less effective.

Chapter Eight

I was learning how I could best help him. Every day was a tightrope to be walked with extreme care. It wasn't easy, but he deserved peace, and I was the one person in the world that could give it to him. I was his comfort, his security: my strength had to be enough for both of us-although I could feel it stretching towards breaking point.

Apart from our evenings in the garden, the only time he wanted to leave the house was to take a late-night trip to the supermarket. He would demand I drive him to the nearest town and wait for him in the car while he wandered the aisles. He didn't want to buy anything, just wanted to be near other people without being afraid that something would be expected of him. I hoped it might do him some good. At least he was out of the house in a normal environment- maybe it would repair his confidence. Once, I made the mistake of leaving the car to join him. He spotted me as I approached and unleashed a look of such ferocity, I turned and fled back to the car. Waited with patient obedience and was rewarded with a silent drive home. Much more comfortable than screaming threats and verbal abuse-I was grateful for the peace.

He wasn't able to work anymore. Spent his days

sleeping in between browsing the internet. He loved online conversation -well, *argument* -and would recount with relish who he'd spoken to, what he'd said, how he'd won the debate. He was aggressively anti-feminist and would actively seek out women to harangue. After one woman -baiting session, he told me how one woman had "mocked him" for being "butthurt." Full of righteous indignation.

"Taking the piss because my dad raped me. Butthurt, get it? Feminist scum." He sneered. "Bitches"

He knew very well that the Americanism "butthurt" meant 'to be unjustifiably offended or resentful.' By being willfully ignorant, he could cast these women as heartless harpies who were so devoid of basic human decency that they would use a victim's experience of abuse to insult and degrade. By extension, all women were disgustingly gleeful at the thought of child abuse. This was a pattern with him-to turn things around to fit his narrative and portray himself as the victim in every scenario. In reality, he was the aggressor.

Before I had been so thoroughly subdued and silenced, I once made the mistake of observing that no matter what I did, *he* was the injured party, and *I* was the one at fault. That comment earned me hours of screeching verbal abuse, delivered at a pitch so deafeningly loud I was afraid he would damage my hearing.

"You think I LIKED being a victim! That I enjoyed what my dad did to me?! You FUCKING BITCH! YOU SICK FUCK!"

followed by further hours of 'restraint' on the kitchen floor after I became 'hysterical' and needed him to 'calm me down.'

It surprised me at first, his misogynistic opinions. He had been abused by men, not women-where did this hate of women come from?

Over time, the origins of this deep-seated loathing became clear. He hated his mother and older sisters for their failure to protect him. Particularly his mother. He'd rage against her for hours. When incensed by thoughts of her, he would listen to John Lennon's 'Mother', nodding his head in agreement as he listened to the familiar lyrics. I guess he was looking for someone who understood how he felt, perhaps feeling less alone when listening to the words of others: words that reflected his own feelings. For his every dark mood, he had a piece of music attached. Far from being a comfort to him, this practice seemed to fuel his gnawing resentment.

He felt that her failure to protect him was the ultimate betrayal – even worse than the violations he had suffered at the hands of his father. Thinking about

55

her seemed to provoke more intense pain-fueled fury than the memory of his father's abuse.

At the age of 15, he had finally found the courage to tell his mother everything. He had expected her to support him. Wrap her arms around him, tell him how sorry she was. Her response had not been the one he was looking for: '*Oh son, that was years ago.*' Realisation hit him hard. *She must have known what his father was doing to him all along.* Unable to fully accept this truth, he had persisted. Tried to talk to her again. And was told sharply '*don't guilt trip me.*'

So, there it was. An abusive father and a mother who was willfully ignorant at best and complicit at worst. Hideous knowledge for a young man to absorb. Hardly surprising then, that he despised her. Loathed her. I could understand that. But his abhorrence for one woman who had failed him festered and grew into a hatred and deep mistrust of all women. And there was I, living with him - a man who loathed women. I became a target for all that hate and mistrust. He was constantly watchful for any signs of betrayal from me. Appeasement became my default setting.

I listened patiently to his violent misogynistic outbursts, learning to feign an air of understanding mixed with contrition. I became a master of the blank expression. The slightest hint of disbelief, incredulity or -God forbid - downright contradiction from me was lethally dangerous. Questioning his views would provoke a towering rage, so I learned not to - no matter how ludicrous his outpourings were. His method of correction - to declare I was becoming 'hysterical' and needed to be 'restrained' to protect me from myself - became an almost daily ordeal for me. This involved holding me down on the floor in painful postures for hours at a time. Being held down by a large, powerful man was without doubt one of the most terrifying things that had ever happened to me. I tried everything I could think of to get away- apart from physically fighting back. I pleaded that I needed the loo, tried to make myself sick…nothing worked. He was immovable. Relentless. I gave up on all attempts to resist, instead turning to another tactic. I'd force my body to become limp in his grip. Took my mind elsewhere: the only escape I had. It's hard to adequately express the feelings of humiliation and weakness that comes from being held down. Such a degrading thing to do to another human being.

His opinions were lifted straight from the manosphere. Contrary to all available evidence, not to mention his own experiences, he would insist that the vast majority of paedophiles were women. He poured over online conspiracy theories, chuckled over viciously anti-feminist 'jokes' and memes. Anything he could find online that justified his hatred of women was enthusiastically consumed, to be regurgitated back at me when I arrived home.

Over time, my own mental health began to erode. The constant fear, increasing control and sleep deprivation took its toll. As I wasn't permitted to move from the bedroom unless it was to go to work, I was unable to keep the house in a livable state. We existed in squalor. The house stank of damp towels, unwashed crockery and the overflowing cat litter tray that poor Cleo was forced to use. Eventually, she gave up on it, preferring to relieve herself in corners and behind furniture. My once beautiful home had become a slum. I was close to losing my will to live.

Strategies I'd used to calm and comfort him stopped working. The kind, gentle, loving man that had joined me in my little home was being overtaken by a much darker personality: hateful, vengeful, spiteful, vicious. His personal anguish was increasing. Any comfort he got from our relationship now seemed to come not from loving me, but from hating me. I'd been naive to believe I could love him better. If anything, my presence seemed to fuel his dark moods. I couldn't help him.

I came to accept that if I wanted to survive, I had to end this relationship and reclaim my life-but how?

Chapter Nine

To the outside observer, the answer would have been obvious. Report him to the police, have him removed from the house and, if necessary, get a restraining order. Job done. If I'd had a friend in the same position, I would have given the same advice. Would even have accompanied her to the police station and sat with her while she gave her statement. I have friends who I'm sure would have done that for me. If they knew.

But ...I was deeply involved with this man. Still thought I loved him. I didn't want him to come to any harm. I wanted desperately for him to find happiness somewhere else. With someone else. To look back on this relationship with fondness. To understand this decision wasn't made because I didn't care about him: It was because I *did*. Perhaps *I* was the trigger that ignited his darkness: unwittingly provoking his cruelty with something I said or did. Or something I *didn't* say or do. Not knowing what I was doing wrong meant I couldn't put it right. What was that old saying – *if you love someone, set them free?* I'd have to explain all this clearly. Make him feel that this wasn't a rejection, but a sacrifice on my part. For his own good. I would break up with him as gently and as reasonably as I possibly could.

Within a 'normal' relationship, this would have worked. Every day, couples went their separate ways after an honest, caring heart-to-heart: why not us? Bruised hearts healed in time – we'd all been there: recovered from broken relationships and gone on to find new ones. The human heart was resilient. It recovered in time. *But would his?*

I waited for one of his calmer days. He still had them, although they were becoming increasingly rare. A day where he let me cook for us, let me eat with him. Perhaps permit me to sit on the sofa with him to enjoy a movie. Like thousands of couples do every day. Nothing special, just normal. Loving.

The day came.

I had rehearsed my words carefully, even practiced them in a mirror: watched my own face as it adopted just the right expression-a mix of sorrow, bravery and sincerity. Would I make eye contact? I'd try. I would have to gauge his mood carefully and let my body language be guided by his reaction.

I took his hand. Gently. Told him we had to talk. This wasn't working. I wasn't happy, and more importantly, I could see he wasn't either. I couldn't give him the peaceful life he deserved, but maybe someone else could. I wasn't strong enough or brave enough. He should be free to find the right woman, yes? It would break my heart, but I knew it was something we had to do. For both of us, but largely for him. I had to let him go. Slowly and clearly, without a trace of indecision, I delivered every carefully considered word. When I had said all that I needed to, I kissed him. Squeezed his hand. And held my breath.

Silence. Anxiously, I scanned his face. Searching for a reaction. Nothing. Not a flicker of emotion. Then, almost imperceptibly, he nodded. Stood up, drew himself to his full height. Pulled me to my feet and into his arms. With my head crushed against his chest, I listened for the tell-tale heightened rhythm of an agitated heart. No anger, no sadness. He hugged me tighter for a moment, then released me, turned and went upstairs.

Flooded with relief, I took a deep breath. Then another. Steadied my nerves. Felt my quickened pulse begin to slow down until my heart was no longer racing. *Was that it? As easy as that*? I wanted to believe.

Silence from upstairs.

I went into the kitchen and busied myself. Emptied the sink of stacked dishes, ran the water. Still silence from upstairs.

Then the sudden shock of a blow to the face. Pain, from the bridge of my nose, spreading across my cheekbones, bringing instant tears to my eyes.

Instinctively, my hands flew to my face where they were met by a trickle of blood. I heard myself scream, then sob. *He wasn't in the room - had he thrown something?* I looked around in panic, searching for the answer. An unopened can of coke was hissing on the floor, spraying its contents from a rupture in its side. *He must have crept down the stairs, hurled the can at my face, then left.*

I sobbed uncontrollably, loudly, gasping for air. All the nervous energy I had so recently subdued in order to get through my speech was released. I howled like an animal.

Then he was in the room with me. Holding me close, shushing me gently. Asking me what had happened.

"you..you..hit…me…the ….can…" between heaving gulps of distress. He was confused, concerned. Incredulous even.' *Hit you? No love…I came into the kitchen, tossed a can into the bin. I'm so sorry it hit you. I didn't mean to…I love you…my sweet baby….its ok…come here….ssshhh…'.*

On and on he went, whispering words of gentle comfort. I listened. Struggled to understand-was it an accident? It must have been…he was being so kind, so considerate.

I allowed myself to be steered into the living room. We sat together and he rocked me like a child until I was able to control myself.

He brought me hot tea, softly chided me for *'getting in the way'* when he was only trying to keep the place tidy. Dabbed at my face with a piece of kitchen roll. Took care of me.

Numbly, I surrendered to his tender ministrations. Limp with exhaustion, I was grateful when he decided it was time we went to bed.

And that was that.

Chapter Ten

Except it wasn't.

I had voiced the desire to leave him and even that, no matter how tenderly I had expressed it, was an act of betrayal. I had done what all women do-proved myself untrustworthy and disloyal, caring only for myself.

From that day, I felt his contempt swell until he was unable to disguise it at all. Or unwilling to. He expressed his loathing verbally, sometimes physically. The physical chastisement was easier to bear than the verbal assaults. It certainly didn't last as long. He could berate me for hours-viciously and loudly, at an ear-splitting pitch. A stream of threats, obscenities, and insults. Once, he told me that I had been responsible for the death of an ex-boyfriend. Apparently, my callous behaviour had caused him to succumb to laryngeal cancer - a particularly cruel inversion of the truth; *'You dumped him, and it made him ill. You really are an absolute bitch. You broke him apart. It's your fault he's dead. Really don't give a shit about anyone else do you...'* Early in our relationship, I'd trusted him with moments of my life that had affected me deeply: the sad times, the happy times. All those confidences had given him material to distort and spit back at me, in order to portray me as an unfeeling, sadistic monster. Perhaps it was an attempt to justify his abuse. Was it just another way to torment me, or did he truly believe I was the terrible person he was describing? If so, *then why wouldn't he leave me?*

There were no kicks or punches, but he continued to 'restrain' me. He would take hold of my wrists and squeeze until I felt my bones would shatter-sometimes leaving fingerprint patterns in vivid red, fading through shades of blue, black, purple, green, yellow and finally into brown. He'd seize me by the shoulders and jolt me backwards and forwards until my neck felt as if it would break.

On one occasion, he shook me so violently that my head snapped backwards, thudding audibly against a wall. When that happened, I saw his eyes widen with shock. There was a flash of something then - was it remorse? Shame? Self-awareness? But it was gone in an instant, replaced with the usual narrow-eyed loathing.

That flash of humanity in his eyes, however fleeting, allowed me to convince myself that the charming, funny, clever and slightly eccentric man I'd met at the railway station was still in there. A genuine part of him, not an act he'd used to hide his true self. But he was becoming increasingly monstrous. The old 'Jeckel and Hyde' cliche was horribly apt-and Hyde looked like he was winning.

His urge to control me was intensifying. Scathing about the job I loved, he hated to hear me talk about my days at work with obvious pleasure. It felt as if he was jealous of anything and anyone else who brought me happiness-whether that was because he wanted to be my whole source of joy, or he wanted me to live in unrelenting misery I wasn't sure. Whichever it was, he made it clear he'd like nothing better than for me to give up work and stay at home with him.

Apart from the distress losing my job would cause me, there was no way we could manage without my wages. He had long ceased any paid employment - as far as I could tell anyway. He made no financial contribution at all. Everything fell to me-food, rent, bills. Everything. And I was beginning to struggle with increasing credit card debt. Some months I could barely make the minimum payment.

He'd make sneering threats about recording my cruelty towards him and sending a copy to my manager. My horrible character would be revealed, and I would be sacked. Considering I was terrified to say anything he even slightly disapproved of, I doubted he could follow through with this threat-unless he could somehow create fake 'evidence'? It felt as if he was actively trying to destroy me. I checked my every word and deed in case he found a way to discredit me in the eyes of others. Or did he genuinely believe I was cruel to him? My mind was constantly working on trying to figure him out- to understand what was motivating him to behave in this way. Was it something I was doing? Or something I should be doing? It made no sense. *He* made no sense.

We had a new morning routine. Every day he would ask me to ring in sick so I could support him at home. He tried threats, tears and tantrums. I resisted. My job was the only piece of my life that was now "normal", my workspace the only place I felt safe. I was determined to hang on to it. One morning, he was particularly determined.

'*He needed me at home. He would die without me. I didn't care. I was a cold bitch. I'd stay if I loved him.*' On and on it went. Still, I resisted. Walked away from him. Went to make myself a sandwich for lunch.

Suddenly, he was behind me. Screaming that I'd threatened him with the knife I was using to butter my bread. He grabbed me violently, tore the knife from my hand. Spun me around to face him and clamped his hand across my mouth. His nails dug into my cheeks painfully as he forced me backwards over the kitchen worktop. My back felt like it was at breaking point, yet he continued to push my upper body whilst pinning my legs with his. With his thumb, he pinched my nose closed. This was the closest he'd yet come to killing me. Would he suffocate me? Pick up the knife? I felt my eyes widen. His face was millimetres away from mine.

Then, he let me go. Began to scream and hit himself. Ran into the front room and curled up in front of the door. There, he continued to scream and rock back and forth, in the foetal position.

I suppose he was waiting for me to run to him, wrap my arms around him and comfort him, just as I had a thousand times before. Instead, I wrenched open the back door and ran. Hurled myself into the car. Locked the doors. Froze as I waited for the heavy thud of his feet as he pursued me. He didn't appear. The door remained firmly closed. Cautiously, I rolled down the window. Listened. He was still screaming. An injured animal. Perhaps the cacophony of screeches he was producing had deafened him to the sounds of my escape.

I drove to work. Parked my car. Flipped the sun visor down and examined my damaged face in the mirror. Blooded fingernail marks were scattered across my cheeks, my eyes swollen with tears I hadn't even realised had been shed. I cleaned myself up, using a whole packet of wet wipes until I was satisfied that the damage would be hard to spot. I applied makeup: blusher to disguise my pallor, lipstick to enhance my forced smile. It took several minutes of deep breathing before I felt able to convincingly feign normalcy. When I felt ready, I went into the building.

After work, I rang the police.

Chapter Eleven

I rang 101 and told the voice on the line what had happened. Sounds crazy, but I wanted to be sure what he'd done was a crime. That I wasn't overreacting. I didn't tell them about everything else he'd done to me, just went through methodically and mechanically what had happened that morning.

"A crime? Yes. It most certainly was. Where can we find him?"

I hesitated…*they were going to arrest him*? No. That couldn't happen. He'd be so afraid. They'd have to drag him out of my house. I imagined how he'd feel…abused by gangs of men as a child then physically overpowered by the police. To see him treated like that…I couldn't bear the thought.

The voice on the other end of the line spoke patiently and slowly, enunciating every word with care.

"Where can we find him. Miss? Stay on the line. Are you at home now?"

"No. I'm still at work." I mumbled.

I heard the disbelief in his voice. *"Could I give him my address?"*

"Look…he's just texted me. He's gone. Left me. I'll OK. I'm safe. Sorry to waste your time."

Before he could press me further, I ended the call.

I drove home.

I sat in the driveway for some time. Thinking hard. Things couldn't go on like this. If I didn't do *something,* something terrible was going to happen, and soon.

We needed help. Not the police-they'd see me as the victim and punish him, I was sure of it. He didn't deserve that. He needed help, and not just mine. I wasn't up to it. I'd failed.

OK. We needed to talk. I went into the house. Quietly.

I'd half expected to find him behind the door where I'd last seen him. He wasn't. Nor was he in the kitchen, or our bedroom.

I found him in the second bedroom-the room I used mainly for storage. He liked to use this room as his personal space and disliked me going in there.

There he was. Sitting hunched over his laptop that lay on my desk, his back towards me, engrossed in whatever he was reading. As I pushed open the door, he snapped the lid down quickly with some force. Rose to face me.

I scanned his expression. Saw he was calm. I was tense, on my guard, but spoke firmly. "We need to talk about this. I'll make you a coffee. Come downstairs."

I thought it'd be safer to talk in the lounge-easier

to get out quickly if I needed to.

I didn't wait for his response, just turned and left the room.

As I waited for the kettle to boil, I gave myself a pep talk. *Stay calm. Make him see sense. Put the case logically. Be brave. This might be our last chance.*

Quietly, softly, his tread giving no indication of aggression, he made his way down the stairs. Watching him from the kitchen doorway, I assessed his body language. Upright posture, unclenched jaw, hands hanging loosely by his sides...a promising start.

I joined him on the couch. Reached for his hand. Took a breath. Here goes.

"I spoke to the police today."

I felt him flinch-his hand in mine tightened its grip.

"What you did this morning-that can't happen again. What you did was a criminal offence. It was abuse. Do you understand?"

He nodded slowly, his expression inscrutable. I continued.

"It can't happen again. I mean it. Next time, I'll make a complaint. That's the last thing I want to do Love...believe me. I love you. But we need to fix this."

His grip on my hand relaxed a little, but not much.

"The first thing we're going to do is talk to a doctor. I've made an appointment. This Friday when I get home from work, we're going straight there."

He gave no response: no agreement, but no outright refusal either.

I was afraid my determination would evaporate if I looked at him, so I'd kept my eyes to the front: fixed on the wall. Now, I turned to look at him.

There was no anger written on his face, no rage in his eyes. He looked…passive? Resigned? I relaxed a little. He regarded me closely, his eyes roving across my face. Checking my resolve perhaps. I smiled gently, reassuringly.

"Things will get better Love. But we must do this."

A slow nod and a look of intense sadness from him. But no words. I took his nod as acceptance and felt relief burst inside me.

The rest of the evening was calm. I ordered a Chinese meal -his favourite. He was quiet, but I filled the empty air between us with chatter about my day at work. At least he ate. That was a good sign, but I was still wary.

Soon, it grew dark. We went to sit in the garden. He lit a cigarette, the sudden flair of the lighter revealing his expression: gentle, sad, a softness that both melted my heart and lent steel to my resolve.

73

This was the real him. Loving, accepting, understanding. I wasn't foolish enough to believe one trip to the doctor would return him to me permanently. I knew it would be a long process-might even involve a stay in hospital. He was very ill. More accurately, he had suffered an injury- an injury that would take patience and care to heal. But he could be helped. All we needed was expert guidance: help and support from people far more skilled and knowledgeable than I.

Stars embedded in the blackness of the night sky drew our gaze upwards, simultaneously lifting both our heads and our hearts. For the first time in a very long time, I felt hopeful.

I heard him murmur:

"*I am not yours, not lost in you,*

Not lost, although I long to be

Lost as a candle lit at noon,

Lost as a snowflake in the sea.

You love me, and I find you still

A spirit beautiful and bright,

Yet I am I, who long to be

74

Lost as a light is lost in light.

Oh plunge me deep in love-put out

My senses, leave me deaf and blind,

Swept by the tempest of your love,

A taper in a rushing wind."

We sat for what felt like hours, in the silence of the night, my head resting on his shoulder, his hand in mine.

The church clock spoke the hour. 1am. I needed to rest.

Not fully trusting him yet, I decided to spend the rest of the night on the couch. Fully clothed, just in case. A night alone in bed would give him time to think and allow me some much-needed respite. And hopefully, some sleep.

He nodded in agreement, wrapped his arms around me in a warm embrace, kissed me softly and went upstairs.

Swaddled in a blanket with Cleo lending her comforting warmth as she settled onto my stomach, I fell almost immediately into a deep and dreamless sleep.

Violent movement snatched me into semi-consciousness. Instant panic, confusion, terror. The couch lurched several feet, coming to a shuddering halt as it found the heavy oak bookcase that stood against the wall. Books, glass vases, assorted pieces of ceramic that had moments before crammed the shelves fell on top of me. Sounds of destruction tore into my ears. The bookcase bent over me at a precarious angle, threatening further assault.

I threw myself into the floor - instantly awake - and scanned the room. Early morning daylight filtered through the curtains. There was no sign of him, only the evidence of destroyed treasures strewn across the room told me he had been there at all.

I didn't stop to find him. Snatching up my keys and phone, I threw myself out of the door and fled to the car.

Once safely locked safely inside, I examined myself for injuries. Forearms screamed in agony, already swelling in reddened lumps. A thin gash spilled blood from the centre of my forehead trailing redly down towards my lip. My hands and knees were peppered with small cuts.

It was 4am. I sat for perhaps an hour, considering my next move. Fortunately, I had packed a 'panic bag' and hidden it in the boot: toothpaste, wet wipes, a change of clothes.

Throughout that hour, my eyes remained fixed on the house. I expected to see him appear-come roaring down the path towards me-but there was no sign of him. No movement at all.

Eventually I was able to drive. The town in which I worked had a twenty-four-hour public convenience built handily next to an open car park. That's where I headed.

By the chilly morning light, I examined myself in the aged beveled mirror that hung over a substantial sink, grateful that I didn't have to repair myself in one of those modern combined wash-and-hand dryers. The silvering had decayed, leaving a damaged reflective surface that distorted my image. The face staring back at me…I barely recognised that poor woman. Her eyes peered back at me from behind half-open lids, smeared with last night's makeup. Crusted blood snaked from her forehead, slid past her nose and lips and ended its journey at her trembling chin. Armed with handfuls of wet wipes, I did my best to repair her.

Washed, dressed, and disguised by long sleeves and makeup I made my way to work.

Another day of doing my best to function without

arousing suspicion. All the while, considering my next move.

Thoughts of returning to the house provoked a bitter bile of terror to rise into my throat. I swiftly rejected the notion.

Call the police? No. He needed to be taken care of by understanding mental health experts, not to be treated like a criminal. He was just as much a victim as I-maybe even more.

I clung to the hope that we would be in a doctor's office by Friday, after which support would be put in place and the healing could begin. We could still have our happily ever after, as long as we put ourselves in the hands of professionals and let them do their job.

I messaged him:

Hope you're ok Love? I'm not feeling great. I'm going to stay at a B&B. I'll see you at the doctors on Friday, around ten to five.

He read the message, as evidenced by reassuring blue ticks, but gave no reply.

I found a nice little B&B that was within my budget, booked in for two nights, and waited for Friday.

Chapter Twelve

The luxury of two night's rest felt like heaven. Only worries for his safety and the dull ache of my swollen, bruised forearms disturbed my comfort. I messaged him frequently:

Are you OK?

See you Friday-just 2 days Love T

Thinking of you x

I'll wait for you outside and we'll go in together. 5pm. Don't forget.

Each message drew no response, but the telltale blue ticks told me he was reading them, and more importantly that he was OK. I was grateful to see them; they reassured me that he hadn't *'done something stupid'*. I forced myself not to return to him, although the urge to do just that was a powerful one. I had to stick to my guns. Break this hideous cycle of '*love-hate'* that we'd fallen into.

My few days at the charming little B&B were restorative. Work was so much easier after a good night's sleep-I felt myself dropping the *'everything's OK'* pretense slightly. I'd underestimated how vital sleep was for mental and physical health; the near constant migraine, the aches and pains, all began to subside.

The room I was staying in charmed me. Decorated

with country cottage prettiness and leaning heavily into 'shabby chic' style, it reminded me of what my own bedroom had looked like just a few short months ago. Fresh, clean sheets and a hygienically sparkling en-suite reminded me of a time when living in comfortable dignity was something I took for granted. Coupled with my temporary break from living in constant watchful fear, the relief of rest carried me a little way back to my old self. Helped strengthen my resolve.

All too soon, I was checking out and driving back to my village. Parking my car next to the curb outside our local doctor's surgery, I waited.

From where I was parked, I had an unobstructed view of my house. Fixing my eyes on the front door, I crossed my fingers; hoping to see it open, watch him walk to meet me, take my hand and sit with me in the waiting room. *Please, please, please. Don't let me down.*

The door stayed resolutely shut, the curtains drawn. No movement. No signs of life.

I checked my watch. 4.55pm.

What to do? I sat and fretted.

I rang him once, twice, three times. Each time the call was rejected. Messaged him - *hello Love, are you coming? I'm outside the doctors.* Blue ticks, but no words.

Disappointment seeped through me, crushing my hopes. I felt deflated, although unsurprised.

4.57pm.

I had no choice. I would have to keep the appointment alone. With one last hopeful glance at the house - still nothing - I hurried to make the appointment on time.

The doctor's office was comfortably sterile. Vases of cheerful daffodils partially obscured informative posters. The air was subtly scented. I inhaled - *lavender? Orange?* A chipped but charmingly decorated bowl on the desk in front of me was the source, filled with purple buds and slices of dried citrus. Chosen to relax patients perhaps. If so, I appreciated the effort. Palms sweaty with nerves, I listened to my heartbeat drumming uncomfortably in my ears.

I was about to tell a complete stranger things that I had kept hidden for a very long time.

She indicated a chair, inviting me to sit. I lowered myself into it, then half-rose to clumsily draw it nearer to her desk, leaning a little closer: conspiratorially.

"I was expecting to see a Mr…." peering at her computer screen.

"Yes" I interrupted "my partner. He's…unwell."

, of course he was. Hence the appointment.

"It's not ethical for me to discuss a patient with anyone other than him. Even his partner." Slightly abrupt. Snippy. Clearly thought I was wasting her time. Perhaps I was.

I tried again.

"He's been unwell for a long time now. I'm…afraid. For him. I'm afraid for him."

"Oh?" Concerned now, a more patient tone. She transferred her attention from the computer to my face.

I chose my words carefully, not wanting to reveal too much of what had happened in the house. Nervous, I spoke quickly;

"He's angry all the time, and very sad. I can't remember the last time he left the house, except to sit in the garden. He's often unsteady on his feet. Spends most of his time lying in bed." Desperately trying to tell her how serious the situation was, without telling her the full story: *he hurts me. He frightens me. Sometimes, I think he wants to kill me.*

"You think he's depressed?"

I nodded.

"Do you think he might take his own life?"

Her bluntness elicited a firmer nod. *Yes, I really thought he might.*"

And where is he now?"

I hesitated. He was at home. *Alone.* I should be

with him.

Reading her face, I could tell that she shared my unspoken thought.

"Can you do anything? Could he be sectioned?"

Her expression told me that that was out of the question.

"That's really only something we can do if he's a danger to himself or to others."

He is. He is dangerous. Still, I couldn't tell her the whole truth.

"I really have to see him in person. Why don't you make another appointment on your way out."

That was it. I was being dismissed. Perhaps prompted by my strained expression, she added "I'll put a note on his record."

Numbly, I left the office. Stopped to make another appointment (a week and a half away) hefted open the surgery door. Walked resignedly towards the house.

I felt defeated. There was very little hope of him attending a doctor's appointment willingly. I couldn't get him help without his co-operation. We were on our own. I would have to go back to the house.

He was lying in my bed; on his left side, facing the wall. Cleo was balanced on his hip, doing the job he had assigned to her: support animal.

Stale body odour hung suffocatingly over the small room. He was wearing the same clothes. No dirty plates or cups had been added to the jumble of crockery that littered the carpet. Unwashed, unfed, unkempt, alone, helpless. He looked as if he had curled up there the moment I left. Had been waiting for me to return.

Was this staged? I wasn't sure. If this scene was staged, it had been convincingly done. However, staged or not, some things were clear. He would make no attempt to get help for himself and was dependent on me to save him. Without me, he would let himself die.

My attempt to get outside help had been fruitless. It couldn't be done. He would need to co-operate, and I knew with cast iron certainty that *that* was out of the question. It could only be done against his will.

I crawled into the bed. Cleo welcomed me warmly, fussing and nuzzling into me. Had she been fed? Poor girl. There was no welcome from him. No response at all. I had nothing to say to him either. What would my next move be? I had exhausted all available options – except for one.

I didn't sleep. I wasn't sure if he did. His breath came in a regular rhythm. No sign of rage-I felt relatively safe, but still wary. Always wary.

Chapter Thirteen

Saturday began surprisingly peacefully. That in itself made me anxious: waiting for the inevitable explosion.

He got out of bed as if nothing out of the ordinary had happened. Didn't wash or change his clothes but left the bedroom and went downstairs in an apparently buoyant mood. I toyed with the idea of raising the topic of our next doctor's appointment but quickly packed the notion away. For now, at least. I'd unpack that conversation after he'd been calm for a couple of days. I was going to take things steady. Ease him into the idea. The appointment was over a week away. I had time. I could take this slow.

Yet another pajama day. We sat huddled together on the sofa; watched a movie, shared a packet of biscuits, drank endless cups of tea. He wanted to play charades, so we did, laughing over his ridiculous grimaces and my hopeless inability to guess the book. Far better read than me with an impressive knowledge of literature, his attempts to communicate in mime the title of books I'd never heard of left me flummoxed.

Evening drew in. We sat in the garden. in the tranquility of early evening twilight, waiting for the stars to join us.

His mood was calm. Reflective. We hadn't yet

talked about my few days away from him, or his failure to attend his doctor's appointment. I was treading water. Afraid that an ill-considered word or gesture from me would provoke a deadly wave; drowning us both.

Silence from him. No poetry or pontifications tonight. Just silence. I was almost enjoying it-perhaps some time to reflect would lead him to the right conclusion: seeking professional help was the way forward. I fervently hoped so.

Finally, he rose, indicating that he was ready to go back inside.

Once inside, I reached for my phone which I'd left charging on the little shelf by the door. It wasn't there. I looked around, puzzled.

"Love, did you take my phone?"

An immediate shift in mood. I froze. Cursed myself for not thinking before I spoke. He turned slowly; jaw tight, brow furrowed.

"Why the *fuck* would I take your phone?"

I closed my eyes. Sighed. There it was.

"I said. Why. The. Fuck. Would . I . Take. Your. Fucking. Phone??!!!"

Each word punctuated by a step closer towards me. For every one of his steps forward, I took one away from him, until I was backed up against the wall. Trapped. He was inches away now: squared up, shoulders back, head inclined downwards. I looked up at him, then felt my legs give way. I sank to the floor and sobbed out my fear and grief and loss of hope. Things were not going to change.

The simmering reached boiling point.

"COME ON BITCH! LET'S DANCE!"

My heaving sobs stopped abruptly. I almost smiled. Sounded like a line stolen from some cheesy gangster flick, I mused. How does he come up with this nonsense?

I felt curiously detached, almost resigned. Emotionally dead inside, the way I'd trained myself to feel whenever he pinned me to the floor. It may have been my mind protecting itself from the paralysing effects of extreme fear. I felt myself to be an outside observer, dispassionately watching the scene as it unfolded with terrifying predictability.

Gripping me by the wrists, he pulled me up into a kneeling position and dragged me across the floor on my knees. I half crawled; half slid after him across the bare wooden floorboards. Holding my head low, eyes on the floor so he couldn't see my face. This seemed to infuriate him further. He roughly hauled me upwards with some difficulty. I was a dead weight, a heavy ragdoll. Unresponsive in his controlling grip.

He propped me onto my feet, where I swayed

unsteadily; looked up at him, dead in the eye. Braced myself, set my shoulders back. Spoke."

Why are you doing this to me?" Beyond fear, I was emotionally numb enough to challenge him.

For a second, he wore a dumbfounded expression. Perhaps a fraction of a flicker of guilt surfaced before sinking back down into the depths, to be replaced by a look simultaneously speechless and enraged.

Then he bit me. Hard. Darted his head forward, gripped the flesh at the edge of my jaw. Held on tight. Increased the pressure until I screamed.

The sound seemed to shock him. He released me, stepped backwards.

I put my hand to my injured face and waited to see what he would do next.

Nothing. Just stood there, in the wreckage of my once beautiful lounge, studying me. Eyes half closed; nostrils slightly flared.

The air crackled with threat. This was, by far, the most dangerous moment of my life. I remained as still as possible, as if confronted by a rabid dog. *Do nothing*, I told myself. *Don't speak. Don't breathe. Don't even blink.*

Seconds dragged by and became minutes. How many minutes, I wasn't sure. It felt like a very long time. Eventually, I saw his eyes revert to something like normal. His breathing slowed from laboured to regular. The rage had subsided. I risked a breath, then another.

"Shall we go up to bed Love?" I whispered gently. "You look sleepy." I feigned a look of concern, attempted a tender half smile.

He nodded.

I led the way, him following slowly. Settled myself carefully on the bed, opened my arms. He sank down next to me, allowed me to hold him, curled up with his head on my chest and one leg pressed down on mine. Hard.

I closed my eyes. He spoke in a low monotone. Straining to catch the words that I'm not sure were even meant for me, I heard:

"Today, I'm going to bash your fucking brains out."

Chilled to the bone, I fought to appear calm. Trying to put him at his ease, I forced a contented, sleepy murmur. With tremendous strength of will, I *made* my body relax, so as not to communicate my terror.

Lying with him in my arms, I thought desperately; trying to think of a way out. To form an escape plan. I was in no doubt that he would do what he said he would. I had run out of time. Incapacitating fear was kept at bay by my determination to survive. Eventually, we were joined by inquisitive daylight stealing into the room, signaling the start of another day.

Was he asleep? His breathing was deep, regular.

I sat up. Carefully.

No movement from him.

I extricated myself. Slowly. Put one foot on the ground.

Still no movement from him.

Inch by silent inch, I edged myself away from him.

Finally, I was out of the bed and on the floor, on all fours.

I crawled out of the room, keeping low in case he woke. Made my way towards the top of the stairs. Stood up. *Ran*.

Almost immediately, I heard him throw himself out of the bed.

Snatching up my keys - mercifully where I'd left them - I wrenched open the front door and threw myself out of the house.

He was clattering down the stairs now, howling like a wounded animal, a sound of outraged fury combined with immense distress.

Shoeless, I propelled my body towards the waiting safety of my car, barely conscious of the hard concrete path my feet slammed against, not stopping to see how close he was. Unlocked the car, wrenched open the door, flung myself inside, scrabbled for the door, pressed the lock. Finally dared to look up, to see where he was.

He was close. Standing beside my car watching me through the window, panting from exertion and emotion. His face bereft of colour, frozen in a terrified rictus.

It took me a few seconds to get my breathing under control. All the while, he regarded me through the window. I saw grief, pain, loss, terrible realisation move across his face.

"Go back inside." I told him. "Go back inside and wait. You'll be safe. I promise."

People were around. We were attracting curious glances. A man made a move towards us, as if to intervene. With a look of intense sadness, he silently pleaded with me before nodding almost imperceptibly and retreating.

Blooded, bruised and barefoot, I drove into town. I'd googled the address of the nearest police station weeks before - just in case - so I knew where I was going.

Chapter Fourteen

Purpose built and apparently designed by an architect whose brief had been 'keep it within budget' the police station was on the edge of town. Long, squat and imposing, with less windows than it probably needed. In order to reach the plate glass double doors, I had a choice between broad stone steps or ramp. I chose ramp. I was too tired for steps.

Mercifully, my bagful of emergency supplies was still in the car, and it included a pair of trainers: at least I wasn't barefoot. Even so, my appearance was disheveled enough to cause the officer manning the front desk to look twice.

With a calm control that masked my agitation, I gave him a brief outline of recent events. He asked to take a seat.

The waiting room was everything you'd expect a police station waiting room to be: devoid of comfort, but clean and efficient. At least there was a toilet. Good. I badly needed to use it.

Illuminated by harsh lighting and smelling strongly of bleach, the tiny room offered no luxuries. What it *did* offer, however, was a floor-to-ceiling mirror. I regarded myself solemnly, turning my face slowly left then right. There was a definite bite mark at my jawline. I had half believed I'd imagined being bitten, but there was the evidence-outlined in blood and surrounded by angry red; already tinged with purple. I leaned towards the mirror, touched the wound gingerly and winced. I looked like I hadn't slept for days. Or brushed my hair. Rolling up my sleeves, I examined fresh swellings, jostling for position with older lesions. The greatest damage seemed to be to my eyes-not physical damage, but damage, nonetheless. I felt that the injury I saw there would take longer to heal than my cuts and bruises.

They were ready for me. I was shown into an interview room. Furnished for function: windowless, whitewashed walls, lino on the floor. Two doors lead into the room, the one through which I had just entered and another, on the other side of a broad laminate-covered desk. Steel framed and solid, easily four feet wide, heavy and designed with immovability in mind. I took a seat, trying to quell my anxiety. Never in my life had I ever had dealings with the police. Nerves fluttered.

On the other side of the desk, the second door opened, and two police officers entered. One made the introductions while the other busied himself opening a large notebook, pen poised, ready to record whatever I had to say.

"Can we start with your name?

I gave them the details they needed: name, age,

address, contact information. All were noted down efficiently.

"Start at the beginning and tell us what happened. In your own time."

Now for the difficult part. I took a breath and a sip of tea from the eco-friendly cup thoughtfully provided by the desk officer.

I resolved to be concise and unemotional. My task now was to report a crime- provide facts that would help the police to do their job. Not to seek comfort and reassurance. This was not a counselling session.

"On Saturday evening, my partner became angry. He dragged me by the wrists across the floor. I didn't try to resist. He pulled me to my feet and bit me - here." I indicated my jawline.

At this point, the interview was stopped, and a camera was brought into the room. My face and forearms were photographed from several angles before I was asked to continue."

He later told me he was going to "bash my fucking brains out." Sorry for the swearing"

A slight smile from the officer sitting opposite.

"The next morning, I ran from the house. He chased me, but I got away. Then I came straight here."

No reaction at all from the other side of the desk, just the scratching of pen on paper.

Put simply and factually, the assault I'd suffered sounded far less terrifying than I had felt it to be. I looked at them anxiously. Was it enough?

No indication. More questions.

"Whose house is it?"

"Mine"

"Do you own it?"

"No. It's rented."

"Does he contribute to the rent?"

"No.Never."

"Is his name on the rental agreement?"

"No."

"Do you want him to leave?"

"*Yes*." Here, I deviated from monotone to earnest conviction. They exchanged a glance.

"Have there been any other incidents like this one?"

"Many."

I was asked to elaborate. Again, I tried to keep it factual. Brief.

"He pins me down. Shakes me. Screams the most awful things at me. Knocks my head against walls and floors. Throws things at me. Traps me in rooms and won't let me leave. Won't let me sleep. He…" I paused "*He frightens me*."

All noted down.

By recapping his pen and placing it on the table,

the scribing officer indicated that they had enough information for now.

"We've had a look at our records. There are five recorded reports of a woman being threatened by a man. We think that you may be that woman."

I blinked. This surprised and embarrassed me. I had thought nobody else knew, but apparently, concerned neighbours had reported what they'd seen. I listened intently as details from the reports were read out.

"A gentleman reported stopping his motorbike to intervene between a man and a woman involved in a violent altercation..."

I remembered the incident.

It was several weeks ago. I had been suffering with the most agonising migraine, lying with a cold wet flannel across my eyes. He had demanded that I drive him to the nearest supermarket. It was late. I resisted, but he would not relent. Eventually, I forced myself to drive. I was in agony, my vision was blurred, my head pulsed with pain. A few minutes into the drive, I had remarked that he was selfish. Cruel. He had responded by screaming and kicking the dashboard. I'd stopped the car, got out and ran. He'd chased and caught me, grabbed me, tried to drag me back to the car. I'd struggled with him - had seen a corner shop was still open, thought if I could get to it, I could ask for help. He had picked me up bodily. I'd struggled and fought against him. At that point, a passing motorcyclist had stopped, stepped off his bike and ran across the road towards us. He had released me immediately, backed away. Snapped instantly back into 'normal' mode. Almost nonchalantly, he had wandered a few steps away and observed us calmly - no sign of the towering fury that had possessed him just seconds earlier. The motorcyclist had spoken directly to me, ignored him – '*was I OK?*

I wasn't OK. Not OK at all. But I'd told him I was. That my attacker was my boyfriend. We were having a disagreement. It had got out of hand. Sorry.

Clearly, the motorcyclist hadn't believed me and had rung the police. I silently blessed him for his attempt to help.

Other kind people had called the police with similar reports, although nobody else had tried to intervene. Reports of me being yelled at, dragged, chased. Pulled out of the car or forced into the car. My neighbours had reported hearing him screaming at me for hours. Later, I learned that the lady next door was looking for somewhere else to live, so frightened and upset was she by what she was hearing through the thin walls separating my home from hers. I was mortified to hear how much we'd disturbed my neighbours; felt tremendous guilt for destroying their peace and quiet. Things like that just didn't happen in our sleepy little village. I was ashamed that I'd brought disruption into other people's lives.

In spite of all these reports, the police had never visited. Never checked on me. This puzzled me, but I guess without the victim's complaint there was very little they could have done. I recalled my first call to the police: *'where can we find him, Miss? Stay on the line. Are you at home now?'* I should have been here sooner.

But I was here now, and I was alive. Safe. Now I needed to get him to a place of safety too.

I signed my witness statement and listened to what would happen next.

I must not go back to the house. They had enough information to make an arrest. They would contact me when they had him in custody to let me know it was safe for me to go home.

My mobile was lost, so I gave my parent's landline as a contact number.

That's where I headed next. To my parents.

Chapter Fifteen

Living in the next village along from mine and both retired, my parents spent their days gardening, walking, reading - enjoying all those activities that working life got in the way of. Painting in my mum's case: beautiful landscapes in oil. An enthusiastic amateur with some talent, she'd had her favourite pieces professionally framed- I had several at home, hung proudly on the walls. Dad had recently got hooked on Nordic walking, spending his afternoons marching up and down the valleys, poles energetically swinging. In short, they were enjoying a happy, peaceful and well -deserved retirement. I was about to disturb that peace.

Guilt and shame made me hesitate and I wondered briefly if I should find somewhere else to stay? But too late. Dad had heard the sound of my car as it pulled into the driveway. He was at the window: puzzled, then surprised, then delighted to see me. It had been a long time. If they were shocked by my appearance, they didn't show it. Placing cups of tea and a plate of those horrible fig roll biscuits that dad was so fond of on the coffee table, they chattered about family stuff: my great aunt's health, a cousin's recent wedding that I hadn't attended, my brother's latest foreign holiday (Tokyo apparently. Alright for some). Listening but not listening, I agonised over how to tell them what had brought me here. Hearing too much detail would be … distressing for them. I was anxious to avoid causing them more upset than was necessary.

The phone rang. Mum answered, listened, then held the receiver towards me.

"For you."

It was the police. They had arrested him, had him in custody. They would be in touch when the decision to charge him or not had been made. For now, it was safe for me to go back to the house. Could I drop a change of clothes in for him?

Of course I would. Thanking them, I replaced the receiver and turned to face my parents. Clearly, they had heard enough to tell them something was seriously wrong.

Breaking with narrative tradition, I started at the end.

"He's in police custody. Arrested today."

I paused. A look of shock and confusion failed to register on either face. What was there though was worried concern.

From the moment I had introduced them to him, they hadn't liked him. My father -observant man that he was - had noticed him using his body to block my interactions with others. Said it looked a lot like control. Instinctively, he had known that this man would not make me happy. Not something I'd wanted to hear, especially at the beginning of the relationship, the giddily romantic starting point. I was angry; *'I wasn't a child for God's sake! And you want to talk about control? Look a little closer to home why don't you?'* Things went downhill from there. I'd stormed out, childishly slamming the front door behind me. This was the first time I'd set foot in their home for months. I hadn't wanted to hear any more criticism of him, so contact with my parents had dwindled to the odd text.

Perversely, I was glad of it. Until I made the decision to save myself, nobody could have persuaded me to leave him. Not family, not friends, not colleagues, no one. Had I maintained contact with my parents throughout the relationship, they would have been in the unenviable position of watching helplessly from the outside. At least they had been spared that.

But now I desperately needed their help and support. Of course, they gave it. Without question. Never once did *'I told you so'* come from them. I wouldn't have blamed them if it had.

With a huge sigh of relief, I gratefully accepted their invitation to stay with them. Moving back into my home was unthinkable. Apart from the fear that the police would release him, the house would take some serious cleaning up before it was livable again. Plus, there were, you know…*memories.*

I had to force myself to drive back to my house. It was the last place on earth I wanted to be.

The door was unlocked, hanging slightly ajar. Surveying the lounge, I felt a rush of embarrassment. Police had been here, seen the utter squalor we had been living in. Shameful.

Cleocatra was curled up on the couch, looking remarkably unconcerned. Pausing to give her a quick tickle under the chin, I made my way to the door that led to the staircase. Stopped dead in my tracks.

A piece of my washing line had been hacked off, tied to the bannisters. His Bluetooth speaker was still balanced on the bottom stair. Images of him choosing music to end his life to rose in my mind. Dreadful mental images of what I could have walked into, alongside the heartbreaking picture of him standing there alone, preparing to....

Right now, he was safe from harm - *but what if the police let him go?* Panic surged. I couldn't call the police to warn them: no mobile. Could I drive back to my parents, use their land line? No. It'd take too long. Taking them two at a time, I hurtled up the stairs, grabbed clothes, toothbrush, shoes, comb, and ran back down the stairs, dodging the makeshift noose as

I flew. Cleo went into her travel box without complaint - perhaps she sensed the urgency of the situation. More likely she was as keen as I was to get out of that house.

Back seat bursting with bundled up necessities, Cleo's box strapped firmly into the passenger seat, my little car made the 20-minute journey in 15. Taking the steps this time, I burst into the police station giving the officer behind the desk one hell of a start.

I dumped my bundle onto the reception desk. Over the heap of jeans, t- shirts, pants, socks, jumpers and jackets, I almost yelled in his face.

"My ex-boyfriend was brought in this morning. He's planning to take his own life. Please. Watch him. He really will. He's not well." I gulped, remembered to breathe. Calmer now "How is he?"

"I'll find out. Just a sec."

He picked up the phone, told whoever was on the other end that I would like a word, and asked me to take a seat.

In no time at all I was joined by one of the officers who'd taken my statement. She motioned for me to follow her and lead the way back into the interview room.

"We arrested your boyfriend..."

"Ex" I interrupted.

"Sorry, ex. He resisted, so I'm afraid we had to

103

restrain him. The plan is to get him to the mental health team. They'll assess him. While that's going on - and it'll take a while, several hours I should think -we'll carry out our investigations."

I blinked. This all felt so unreal -had it only been a few short hours since I ran from the house? So much had happened. Suddenly, I felt completely drained.

"Has he said anything?"

"He has. He said he didn't bite you. It was a kiss."

I looked at her, baffled "*A kiss?*"

"Yes, a kiss" she nodded "He thinks you may have mistaken his moustache touching you for his teeth."

I sighed, nodded. Rolled my eyes a little. Sounded like something he'd say.

"And the bruises on my arms?"

"Those happened as he was fending you off. He was trying to defend himself. Against you."

Wow. That old chestnut. Well, at least that was believable. But the '*teeth were a moustache*' thing? *A moustache that left a mark*? That was just…bonkers. I guess he was so used to me pretending to believe every word that came out of his mouth he thought others would too. Or perhaps he hadn't realised how hard he had bit me: hard enough to leave me blooded and bruised. Hard enough to leave clear evidence.

A memory came to mind, something he'd said back in the early stages of our relationship –'*my ex*

*blamed me for breaking her arm. She attacked me,
and I had to fend her off...'*

I closed my eyes- stupid, stupid woman! Right
from the start, he'd been waving more red flags than
the Danish Olympic team during the opening
ceremony! I felt foolish and angry. Very angry.

Every time I'd believed him in spite of myself (or
made myself believe), every time I'd ignored the
evidence right in front of me, swallowed his bullshit
time and time again-all of it hit me square in the face
with a big fat slap.

Clearly, he had no plans to be honest, to accept
what he'd done. Still casting himself as 'victim' not
'aggressor.' He would never accept responsibility.
Never change. If charged, there would be very little
chance of him pleading guilty. Would that mean a
court case? Me having to be there, give evidence, *see
him?*

I swallowed. Fear fluttered, twisting my stomach
and bringing a wash of cold sweat. My default
position over so many months. Familiar and
exhausting.

That was a bridge to cross further down the line.
Right now, I was going to walk out of this building,
go home-well, to mum and dad's - and put my life
back together.

"We'll keep you informed."
I walked away.

Chapter Sixteen

Luckily, it was end of term. Easter break. Two weeks to pull myself together. Both physically and mentally, I was not in good shape. The last few years had taken an enormous toll on my health; physical and mental.

The first step was simple. Sleep. Exhaustion had been my constant companion for such a long time - I barely remembered what it meant to feel properly rested.

In the quiet comfort of my parent's spare bedroom, my body fell into a death-like stupor of sleep. My mind? Not so much. I was plagued by nightmares, too exhausted to be woken by them. I suffered through horrific images as they flooded my sleeping mind, re-lived over and over my panicked flight from the house. Dreamt I was trying to get through a locked door; unable to find the key. When eventually I *did* wake, I would find myself in a state of confusion: unsure of what was real and what was imagined.

When the police called me with the promised update, I had been almost resentful. I badly wanted to put all this behind me, and any news of him dragged me back into the old mindset: worry for him, an urge to protect, to offer comfort. I was determined not to return to that.

Firstly, the mental health team had made their

assessment, and, in their opinion, he was not a candidate for hospitalisation. I'd furrowed my brow at that - in my opinion, he needed to be sectioned and given some intensive care. He had insisted he would be fine, promised that he'd attend counselling. I knew he wouldn't. Even now, he was refusing to co-operate, to accept help.

Secondly, he had been charged with assault, bailed and housed in a bail hostel. The police had spoken to my neighbours (mortifying!) who had confirmed all that I had said. And more.

He'd told the police that he intended to come back to my house - I gasped at that -insisting he had a '*right*' to live there because he'd been a resident for months.

"We made it very clear to him that that's not how the law works. He has absolutely no legal right to your home. We told him that he's not welcome there anymore."

Not welcome anymore. I felt a pang at that. That must have hurt him badly.

"We've told him not to go anywhere near you. If he does, we'll arrest him." a pause "We thought you'd be pleased to hear that."

The police had clearly done their very best to protect me from him. Perhaps I hadn't sounded as relieved as they'd imagined I would be.

Throughout this whole process, I'd felt the police had focused very strongly on protecting the victim. Me. Which is exactly how it should be, of course. And I was grateful for the way they'd handled things. But yet... a small voice in my head asked *what about him?*

I'd heard from a well-meaning neighbour that she'd witnessed his removal from my house; had spoken to one of the arresting officers. She told me the officer commented; '*c*rocodile tears. *We've seen it all before.*

On hearing that, I'd walked away from the conversation. The scene that I'd pictured weeks before – the one that had stopped me reporting him – was what had happened to him in the end. He had been dragged from my house in tears. My heart broke for him.

At least now, he had somewhere to live and support from mental health professionals -albeit on his terms. I had to be content with that.

Returning to the slow process of recovery, I forced myself to put him out of my mind and concentrate on myself. I had barely survived this relationship. Now I needed to give myself the love and support that I had tried so hard, for so long, to give to him.

The luxury of a couple of pajama days went some way to restoring my spirit and energy. By day three, I felt the need for fresh air and exercise.

A short circular walk, one I'd taken many times with my still very much missed dog, could be found in the village. I set off.

The day was a cold one: the sky grey, the air damp with light drizzle. My feet found the familiar path and I walked quickly, with purpose. I needed the exercise-what was that old saying-healthy body, healthy mind? *Mens sana in corpore sano.*

Unable yet to enjoy the springtime beauty that surrounded me, I watched my feet as they negotiated the rough lane leading down to the river. Kicked the odd stone into hedgerows, until I disturbed a bird into sudden flight. A magpie. I scanned for a second bird, but no. He was flying solo, smart in black and white, accessorised by iridescent purple-blue trim to tail and wings.

"Sorry!" I snapped into a smart salute. I really didn't need any more bad luck – I'd had more than my fair share.

To my right, an ancient style set into the dry-stone wall separated the path I walked on from the path that led down towards the river. As I scrambled over, I paused to trace my fingers over the fossilised branch trapped in the uppermost stone. A smile of remembrance momentarily transformed my expression. I remembered being here years ago with my dad; being lifted up onto this top step where I'd made the exciting discovery. I had listened in fascination as he explained the process of fossilisation. It had intrigued me, the idea of a once living thing leaving such a perfect memento of life behind. This discovery had kickstarted my childhood obsession with fossils, prompted many happy family outings to nearby Saltwick Bay. We'd spent hours hunting for small traces of lives lived thousands of years before ours. I still had some of those treasures: ammonites in the main, curled spirals of solid shell. I remembered how my small fingers had traced those perfectly preserved coils: starting at the centre of each spiral, circling slowly, bumping across each inflexible ridge.

With a fond pat, I left the style and made my way down, towards the sound of crashing water.

Each season brought a different character to the river. Spring and summer warmth saw tranquil waters which lapped almost gently across the riverbed. Tiny fish could be observed in shallower parts-submerged silver-grey clouds of joyous dance: a cast of thousands. Assorted waterfowl- ducks, moorhens, the occasional swan- trailed long knotted ropes of young behind them, seeming oblivious to the frantic efforts their offspring made to keep up. Herons waded at the edge of the waterway in statuesque beauty, still as death but ready to burst into life if an unsuspecting duckling strayed too far from the safety of its family.

Autumn and winter robbed trees of their foliage, leaving the river naked and vulnerable-somber in deathly slumber. Colours were muted then- browns, blacks, greys- none of the vibrant green seen during the warmer months. Trees dressed in mossy tweeds would crowd the riverbank: stooping old men mournfully examining the loss of their youth in the mirror of scarcely moving water. Barely any birds to be seen in the colder months, just a few lonely ducks picking at the riverbed, hoping to find enough food to keep themselves alive.

Today I could feel that the return to summer warmth was imminent. Recent heavy rains had left the river swollen and raging. The path was fenced in, keeping walkers and cattle apart, forcing me to tread perilously closely to surging water. I trod carefully, occasionally hanging onto the fence for added stability. New buds burst from their winter hiding places. Life was returning. As certain as the seasons, peace would soon replace this furious raging. The air was heavy with the promise of a better tomorrow. I swallowed it greedily, reveling in the certainty of rebirth.

On the way back home, my stride was far more buoyant than it had been when I'd set out. I felt lifted;

reinvigorated. More hopeful than I had felt for a long time.

As I passed, a sudden '*chak-chak-chak*' rattled from the deep leafy cover of a hedgerow, provoking a disproportionate jolt of fear to thrum through me. Twin flashes of black-and-white plumage burst from the bushes and chittered away into the long grass. Two magpies. I grinned with relief and felt a sudden rush of happiness.

Back home, I swung open the door, kicked off my wellies and was greeted by my mum holding out the phone.

"Call for you Love. Police."

Chapter Seventeen

"Hello? Yes, speaking. No, I'm not at my home address right now-I'm staying with my parents." I glanced at my mum, who nodded and smiled "indefinitely."

The voice at the other end of the line spoke low, urgently.

"We need to speak to you immediately-what's your current address?"

An icy certainty gripped me. I spoke with care.

"I know what it is you've come to tell me. He's gone."

A pause.

"I'm afraid we really need to talk to you. In person."

I didn't need to talk to them. He had taken his own life. I knew it. The knowledge drained every drop of hope from me, to be replaced by all-consuming grief.

Mum took the phone from my unresisting fingers. I heard her give the officer her address.

It had arrived- the day I'd prayed would never come. I had not one single doubt that that's what the police were going to tell me.

I didn't want this news. Didn't want to know how or when. The *why* I knew already. He'd felt alone and abandoned. Rejected. Unloved. Utterly lost with nobody to turn to. So, he'd left us. Taken himself away, somewhere where nobody could reach him or hurt him ever again. Guilt swelled, the '*what if, if only I'd...*' thoughts began their tormenting refrain in a steady, deafening chant. Overwhelmed, I felt kind hands steer me gently into the lounge.

Soon, the police arrived.

I spoke desperately, panting with grief, guilt, despair.

"Don't tell me how he did it." I was pleading with them "I can't know, I can't have that in my head…"

A booklet was placed in my hands. I looked down. *"Advice and guidance for the bereaved and other victims of incidents on the railway."*

I stopped resisting. They were going to tell me, and I was going to listen. Whether I wanted to or not.

Very early that morning, around the time I was waking up and contemplating what to have for breakfast, he had walked to a spot known locally as The Iron Bridge. A lonely spot: nobody around, especially at that time in the morning. Waited for the early train. As it rounded a corner, heading for the bridge, he'd jumped. The driver had no chance to stop.

There was more information. Much, much more. I felt myself close down: just a handful of words penetrated the fog of grief that overwhelmed me:

coroner, investigation, counselling, support, condolences…

At last, they were gone.

My brain hissed with the hideous knowledge. *There'll be nothing left of him.*

I retreated to bed: raged, sobbed, howled out pain that had embedded itself deep inside. Cried out a stream of unconnected words '*no,no,no, come home, come home, it's ok, I'm here, come home…*

I had survived so much, but this…I felt as if I would never recover.

But there was a tiny spark, operating outside me, urging me to get help. Survival instinct perhaps. Picking up the phone, I made a call to the doctor's surgery-' *my partner killed himself this morning*' - and was told to come in straight away.

God bless that kind doctor. She must have postponed other appointments so she could be there to greet me as I walked into the surgery. Guided me gently into a small, private room. Listened to me as I talked and talked and talked…. sometimes incoherent, sometimes lucid: a torrent of emotion, pouring out unchecked. I know now that this was a nervous breakdown. A complete emotional collapse. She recognised it as such and let me cry, rage, scream until my voice gave out. Finally, when I subsided, exhausted and heaving for air, she reached for my

116

hand and spoke with tender care:

"My dear. You were in an abusive relationship."

I recognised her meaning: *you are not to blame*.

It would be weeks before I believed that. For now, I was being eaten alive by guilt.I was signed off indefinitely: told to take my time and return to work when I felt well again.

Well again…she knew I would get better. In time. Her judgement reassured me. I would be well again. In time.

Weekly appointments were arranged, with strict instruction to come back sooner if I felt I needed her.

God bless that kind doctor.

Chapter Eighteen

Over the following weeks, I was moved and comforted beyond measure by the kindness shown to me by friends, family and colleagues; some of whom I hadn't seen for a very long time.

My parents took on their roles of care givers unconditionally. It must have been hard for them, watching me in pain, but they never crumbled, never made me feel like I was a burden. Comforts, both emotional and material, were provided with endless patience. At times, I'm sure they felt as if I had regressed to a state of helpless infancy.

I recognised my extreme good fortune in having them. I was also lucky enough to have a wonderful circle of friends who rallied around as soon as they heard what I'd gone through. What I was *still* going through.

Carol was one of the first to arrive at my doorstep. She had been hurt and confused by my silence since that day at her smallholding; I'd been too afraid to keep in touch, afraid of more screaming accusations about Dan. I'm ashamed to say I had 'ghosted' her. Blocked her from my social media, ignored her messages until she'd finally given up on reaching out. Had she known what was happening to me, I have no doubt she would have fought like a tigress to get me away from him. Probably part of the reason I'd turned away from her. It wouldn't have taken her long to see that all was not well. But not even my dear, determined friend could have saved me before I was ready to be saved.

She took me back to her beautiful, lively home for a few days. With friends and neighbours dropping by, it was a busy environment. To be honest, I found it overwhelming to be surrounded by so many people. I needed occasional solitude. She gave me my space. Didn't pry when I took myself off to scratch Squealer's broad back alone. Didn't try to 'cheer me up' when I wept. Sometimes, she wept with me.

Another dear friend- Lucy- turned up with the sweetest gift for me - a cushion, all flamingoes and pom-poms, tightly packed with feathers and good wishes. I still have it. With warm-hearted magnanimity, she gave me her day off work for weeks to take me for long walks in restorative nature. Sometimes we shared long conversations, sometimes we were silent. Whatever I needed, she provided.

Alice was another generous friend, giving me a set of keys to her home, allowing me to come and go as I pleased while she was away on holiday. Somewhere to stay when I needed complete solitude- or rather, needed to give my parents a little respite from the relentless grief that I couldn't help but express.

I was scooped up so many times by so many people given companionship and support. Never made to feel I had to talk if I didn't feel able.

Well-meaning professionals tried to arrange counselling for me. I recall the coroner, alarmed by my incoherent howls of distress in the phone, insisting that I visit an excellent councilor he knew. He emailed contact details and recommendations – all of which I ignored. When I stopped taking his calls, he even rang my parents: tried to persuade them to do all they could to get me to make an appointment. I resisted. My doctor made the same suggestion, but didn't press me when I shook my head. At the time, I was resentful, interpreted his suggestion as intrusion. Now, I know it was an act of kindness, prompted by compassion. I'm sure counselling can be an absolute life saver for many people in pain, but I was being so well supported by my wonderful circle of family and friends, I really didn't feel the need to talk to a stranger.

Whole groups of people – some I knew well, others casual acquaintances – banded together in support of me. My social calendar had never been so full. I was invited out for meals, to the theatre, trips to the seaside ... all to keep me busy and to help me rejoin Life. Some of the events I was invited to felt overwhelming. I remember a group trip to the races.

Surrounded and jostled by exuberant racegoers, the thunderous rhythm of hooves on turf matched my anxious heartbeat. I was frightened. I found myself reaching for the reassuring warmth of his hand, wanting to climb back inside our happy little bubble. With him. It was a long time before that feeling of intense vulnerability subsided. But hiding away from people wouldn't have helped me recover. My instinct may have been to hibernate away, nursing my grief and broken spirit, but following that instinct for solitude may have left me unable to fully enjoy life again. I allowed myself the occasional wallow in despair, but I didn't let it go on for too long. Nor did the people around me. I'll be forever grateful for their kindness and support. People must never underestimate the power of kindness. It literally saves people. It saved me.

I was scooped up so many times by so many people; given companionship and support. Never made to feel I had to talk if I didn't feel able.

I found comfort in communicating with strangers online, people who had survived traumatic events similar to my own. I joined a survivor's forum and would go there whenever I felt hopelessly overwhelmed. Sharing experiences with other men and women made me feel far less alone. Less of an oddity. Less *stupid*. Stories similar to my own showed me that these things happened to all kinds of people. It didn't happen to just one type of person. It happed to rich and poor, young and old, introverts and extroverts, all races, all religions or none, all shapes, sizes...it could happen to anyone. The only thing that victims *do* have in common is that they have done nothing to deserve abuse. **Nobody** deserves to feel so utterly dominated and oppressed, so dehumanised by another person that their entire being becomes broken.

I also learned that there are recognised abuser tactics - as if a horrible handbook exists, that abusers consult before carrying out their campaigns of terror. A 'How To' guide for ways in which to dominate, manipulate and terrify others into submission. I discovered new words: gaslighting, love bombing, negging, coercive control, DARVO. I recognised these techniques - He'd used them all: sleep deprivation, social restriction, emotional manipulation, violence. All weapons in an arsenal of abuse and all deployed against me. Learning about these 'abuser techniques' helped me make sense of his behaviour. As an example, when I learned that an abuser often feels a 'shared identity' with his victim, I suddenly saw our 'happy little bubble' in a totally different light. Apparently, an abuser often sees his victim as an extension of himself; is driven to do all he can to prevent her having a separate life. The 'happy little bubble' fantasy that I had found so romantic was actually him attempting to shackle me. To lose my identity and become an extension of him. Nothing more. He was so successful in this that I thought it was love. I *felt* loved. But that's not what it was.

I devoured academic articles on the effects of abuse. Learned that victims often suffer confusion. Lose the ability to trust their own perceptions. Experience severe emotional distress, anxiety, numbness. Descend into depression. That they may be confused about what they think, feel or want, Victims can be left unable to fully understand the danger that they are in.

If they *are* able to escape the relationship, survivors often suffer from psychological damage- damage that could easily be diagnosed as specific mental health disorders: PTSD, depression, personality disorder. These conditions are wounds - inflicted by violence, in the same way a physical injury is caused by assault. I read and digested that these reactions are *normal*. And very understandable. And like a physical injury, they can heal.

The more I learned about post abuse struggles, the more I understood my own mind. Viewing poor mental health as a wound really resonated with me. I *felt* wounded. I repeated to myself *wounds heal*. The recommend four ingredients for recovery: support, validation, understanding, time, I had in place. I would be well again.

My thoughts returned to my abuser. He had suffered the same wounds as I, but his had been inflicted during early childhood. His infant mind had been completely defenseless, whereas I had been abused during robust adulthood. Small wonder then that his injuries had run far, far deeper than my own. I recalled the many times I'd tried to comfort him as he wept and railed against the whole world. I would hold him, tell him he had been injured, but now I was there to help him. '*It's an injury, Love. You've been badly hurt. You'll get better. I'll help you.*'

I had been naive. Underestimated how damaged he was. But I had tried, recognising too late that he needed someone far better equipped to help him than I. Actually, I'm not sure that even the most knowledgeable mental health expert could have healed him completely. Certainly, he himself believed he was beyond saving. But I wish he'd tried.

I'd always believed that happiness lies in other people. I think it was Paramahansa Yogananda who said "The happiness of one's own heart alone cannot satisfy the soul; one must try to include, as necessary to one's own happiness, the happiness of others."

Communicating with others who were living through dark times was restorative, the simultaneous giving and receiving of tender care tremendously healing.

Several weeks passed before the doctor broached the subject of my return to work.

"It might be time to get back to some normality." She'd said, "Back to where you were before."

I nodded slowly.

"You will feel ready one day. Only you can decide when that is."

Finally, I was ready. With care and understanding, I was supported back into work. My manager treated me with such kindness and compassion that I was able to build up to full time attendance within weeks. I was told to take things steady. Not to put myself under undue stress. I certainly felt no pressure from senior management; just kindness and understanding. Being back within a busy working environment- one that I loved – brought me ever closer back to my old self.

Initially anxious, I was back in the old routine within days. One of my greatest fears had been that someone would make a thoughtless remark- not an adult, but a child. I work with young people, and they can be tactless. Tactless without intending to be so – it's just that they are naturally inquisitive. And honest. I was afraid I would react with tears to an innocent, curious enquiry. But it didn't happen. Once, a boy earnestly told me he was sorry for my loss, but that was it. I live and work in a small community- what happened to me must have been common knowledge, especially as the police had questioned my neighbours. But it was never alluded to at work. This was a huge relief. Part of the pleasure of returning to my job was the distraction it offered. And the normalcy.

Initially, I received regular updates from the coroner. Each call left me distraught, to the point I asked him to stop contacting me. It was an unwelcome intrusion into my return to living, potentially delaying my recovery.

He was gone, and no amount of information would change that. He was beyond my help now-why torture myself with knowledge of his injuries? Or the events directly before and after his death? I wanted - *needed* - to distance myself from the horror of it all.

Chapter Nineteen

Eventually, I had to go back to the house and begin the lengthy process of repairing my broken home.

Armed with hundreds of scourers, cloths, bin bags and bottles of bleach, I got to work removing all evidence of the months I'd been forced to live in degrading filth. I worked alone, not wishing to put the evidence of how I'd been living in front of anyone I cared for. It was a distressing process, one that I could never have attempted directly after his death. I wouldn't have been able to confront the evidence of my ordeal without putting my recovery in jeopardy.

Tackling the task one room at a time, it was days before I made my way upstairs.

Stepping into the bedroom, I stopped in my tracks, transfixed by the sight of our bed.

The place where he once lay held visible signs of him. The pillow indented with the shape of his head, the bunched up quilt undulated with hills and valleys that echoed the shape of his limbs. I stared for a very long time, feeling the sting of recently healed wounds reopening. That bed held what was perhaps the last physical evidence that he had ever been here at all. It was indescribably painful.

I was reluctant to strip the bed. It felt as if I was erasing him. But I had to do it. And do it quickly.

Quilt, pillows, sheets, all were bunched up and crammed into the largest refuse sacks I had been able to find. Ready for the tip.

Amongst the pillows, I found one of his beanie hats. My hands reached for it, picked it up gently - almost reverently- and held it up to my face. I remembered the hours I'd spent, staring at the back of his head, trying to gauge his mood. My eyes had traced these knitted cables many times: as familiar as the veins on the backs of my hands. I breathed in deeply. It still smelt of him. Grief overwhelmed me. I lay on the bed and surrendered. Stopped fighting for a little while.

It took all my strength to get up. To drop the hat into the bag with the rest of his bedding. Knot the bag tightly. Say goodbye all over again.

Finally, the room was cleared.

I made my way to the spare bedroom. He had been ferociously territorial about this space, demanding that it be reserved for his exclusive use with no intrusion from me.

The room contained a single bed, desk, chair, drawers and wardrobe. Resisting the urge to bury my face in his clothing, I hastily thrust it all into the waiting bags. Delving deeper into tangles of clothing, towels, sheets, my hand closed on a large glass bottle. I drew it out from its hiding place. Whisky. Drained of its contents. In total I unearthed over thirty empty bottles. Whisky mostly, with the occasional vodka. Yet another deception, another battle he had been fighting that he had chosen to keep from me. I remembered the late night trips to the supermarket. His insistence that I stay in the car while he visited the store alone. Not an example of eccentricity at all, but a calculated deception. I was suddenly weary. How many more lies would be revealed? Anger flared briefly, then subsided, to be replaced by resignation. And pity.

Such a skilled liar. Drinking heavily and keeping it a secret – why hadn't I noticed? Surely there would have been signs – unsteadiness, the whiff of alcohol on his breath, mood swings, insomnia...Ah. There *were* signs. I just hadn't wanted to see them. Yet another example of my willful ignorance. A voice hissed in my head :*he was drinking to cope with his pain...you didn't notice....your fault, your fault, your fault...*No! Not fair at all. He was duplicitous about his drinking, and so many other things.

A cold suspicion slid from its hiding place. *Was he being truthful about his childhood?* I gasped as if doused by iced water. Couldn't even permit myself to contemplate the possibility. *Nobody* could manufacture such horrific details and present them as fact. It simply wasn't possible. *The teeth thing?*

Removing them with plyers? That seem real to you? Wouldn't somebody have noticed? I frowned. Thought deeply...No. Just no. He was mentally damaged by *something.* That much I was certain of. People like me, people who had only ever experienced loving care throughout their childhood, struggle to believe that monsters are real. Monsters who prey on innocent children. That's how these vile abusers are able to conceal their crimes, sometimes for years. Disbelief that this appalling behaviour was humanly possible. As a society, we must do better for our children. We must believe the victims- just as I must believe him.

The desk was a chaos of torn paper, dried-up cups of coffee and overflowing ashtrays. Scooping up the wrecked evidence of how he'd spent his days, I took shallow breaths through my mouth. The combined stench of stale cigarettes and coffee dregs assaulted my nose. I did my best to block it out.

Another discovery. Scrawled across the back of an envelope -a few brief lines in his beautiful flowing handwriting.

Don't leave me. I'm not a bad man. I would never hurt you.

But he had. He had hurt me. Over and over. In many different ways. Did he believe he hadn't? Had he written this to convince me? Or to convince himself?

I remembered how terrified he had been of becoming a man like his father: a man who behaved with unspeakable cruelty towards those he should have loved and protected. Was this note an attempt to alter reality in some way? Did seeing this lie written clearly somehow turn it into truth for him? Or was it simply yet another attempt to emotionally manipulate and confuse me?

I imagined the police outlining the case as they charged him with assault. Putting the evidence in front of him-my statement alongside statements from bystanders who had witnessed his behaviour. Photographs of my injuries, inflicted by him. Being placed in a bail hostel, alongside others who had committed criminal acts. Surely at that point it became impossible to continue living in denial? Did he, in that moment, see himself as a reflection of his father? His greatest fear, come to fruition...

Yet more questions that could never be answered. I closed my eyes. I had to stop. Stop the self-harm of asking myself endlessly: *was it my fault? Could I have saved him? Did I try hard enough? Why wouldn't he save himself? Access the support that was there,ready to help him? Did he hate me? Did he love me? Why did he lie to me? Why,why,why?*

Pointless, damaging, tortuous questions. I turned

131

away from emotion and towards logic. Thought of all I'd learned about abusers and the abused. He was gone. No amount of looking for answers could change that cold certainty.

There was no changing the past. If I hung onto it, I wouldn't survive.

I stood in the wreckage of that room, surrounded by bin bags full of evidence that he was once here, and made a promise to myself. I would let him go.

I left the house, and I never returned.

Chapter Twenty

Some years have passed since I stood in that room, saying my final goodbyes. It took a long time, but I am repaired. Life is good again.

It's true that time heals all wounds. Time and kindness and love.

Never underestimate the good you can do with kindness. Without it, I might not have survived

I no longer attack myself with the *why,why,whys* or wade into guilt. I can't risk drowning. But I do allow myself to remember. Sitting peacefully with Cleo curled up on my lap, my mind sometimes turns towards him. I don't dwell on the terrible things he said and did. I think of the man I met under the railway clock all those years ago. The man he was supposed to be. The man who was so badly damaged that a terrible darkness overtook him; replacing him with a monster.

He had humour and intelligence and just a hint of eccentricity. And he was broken beyond repair at the age of three.